ECDL

for Microsoft Office 2000

CW00767706

Presentations

ECDL3

for Microsoft Office 2000

Brendan Munnelly and Paul Holden

Presentations

*Everything you need to pass the European
Computer Driving Licence*, module by module*

Prentice
Hall

An imprint of **Pearson Education**

London · New York · Sydney · Tokyo · Singapore ·
Madrid · Mexico City · Munich · Paris

PEARSON EDUCATION LIMITED

Head Office:
Edinburgh Gate
Harlow CM20 2JE
Tel: +44 (0)1279 623623
Fax: +44 (0)1279 431059

London Office:
128 Long Acre
London WC2E 9AN
Tel: +44 (0)20 7447 2000
Fax: +44 (0)20 7240 5771

Website: www.it-minds.com

This edition published in Great Britain in 2002
First published as part of ECDL3 *The Complete Coursebook for Microsoft Office 2000*

© Rédacteurs Limited 2002

ISBN 0-130-35463-5

British Library Cataloguing in Publication Data
A CIP catalogue record for this book can be obtained from the British Library

All rights reserved; no part of this publication may be reproduced, stored in a retrieval system, or transmitted in any form or by any means, electronic, mechanical, photocopying, recording, or otherwise without either the prior written permission of the Publishers or a license permitting restricted copying in the United Kingdom issued by the Copyright Licensing Agency Ltd, 90 Tottenham Court Road, London W1P 0LP. This book may not be lent, resold, hired out or otherwise disposed of by way of trade in any form of binding or cover other than that in which it is published, without the prior consent of the Publishers.

'European Computer Driving Licence' and ECDL and Stars device are registered trademarks of the European Computer Driving Licence Foundation Limited. Rédacteurs Limited is an independent entity from the European Computer Driving Licence Foundation Limited, and not affiliated with the European Computer Driving Licence Foundation in any manner.

This book may be used in assisting students to prepare for the European Computer Driving Licence examination. Neither the European Computer Driving Licence Foundation Limited, Rédacteurs Limited nor the publisher warrants that the use of theses modules will ensure passing the relevant examination.

Use of the ECDL-F approved Courseware logo on this product signifies that it has been independently reviewed and approved in complying with the following standards:

Acceptable coverage of all courseware content related to ECDL syllabus Module 6 version 3.0. This courseware material has not been reviewed for technical accuracy and does not guarantee that the end user will pass the associated ECDL examinations. Any and all assessment tests and/or performance based exercises contained in these Modular books relate solely to these books and do not constitute, or imply, certification by the European Driving Licence Foundation in respect of any ECDL examinations. For details on sitting ECDL examinations in your country please contact the local ECDL licensee or visit the European Computer Driving Licence Foundation Limited web site at http://www.ecdl.com.

References to the European Computer Driving Licence (ECDL) include the International Computer Driving Licence (ICDL).

ECDL Foundation Syllabus Version 3.0 is published as the official syllabus for use within the European Computer Driving Licence (ECDL) and International Computer Driving Licence (ICDL) certification programmes.

Rédacteurs Limited is at http://www.redact.ie

Brendan Munnelly is at http://www.munnelly.com

10 9 8 7 6 5 4 3 2 1

Typeset by Pantek Arts Ltd, Maidstone, Kent.
Printed and bound in Great Britain by Ashford Colour Press, Gosport, Hampshire.

The Publishers' policy is to use paper manufactured from sustainable forests.

Preface

The European Computer Driving Licence (ECDL) is an internationally recognized qualification in end-user computer skills. It is designed to give employers and job-seekers a standard against which they can measure competence – not in theory, but in practice. Its seven Modules cover the areas most frequently required in today's business environment. More than one million people in over fifty countries have undertaken ECDL in order to benefit from the personal, social and business advantages and international mobility that it provides.

In addition to its application in business, the ECDL has a social and cultural purpose. With the proliferation of computers into every aspect of modern life, there is a danger that society will break down into two groups – the information 'haves' and the information 'have nots'. The seven modules of the ECDL are not difficult, but they equip anyone who passes them to participate actively and fully in the Information Society.

The ECDL is not product-specific – you can use any hardware or software to perform the tasks in the examinations. And you can take the seven examinations in any order, and work through the syllabus at your own pace.

This book is one of a set of seven, each dealing with one of the ECDL modules. While each book can be used independently, if you are new to computers, you should read Module 2, *Using a Computer and Managing Files* before, this one. Module 2 teaches you the basic operations that are needed in the other practical modules.

The examples in these books are based on PCs (rather than Apple Macintoshes), and on Microsoft software, as follows:

- Operating system: Microsoft Windows 95/98
- Word Processing: Microsoft Word 2000
- Spreadsheets: Microsoft Excel 2000
- Databases: Microsoft Access 2000
- Presentations: Microsoft PowerPoint 2000
- Information and Communication: Microsoft Internet Explorer 5.0 and Microsoft Outlook Express 5.0

If you use other hardware or software, you can use the principles discussed in this book, but the details of operation will differ.

Welcome to the world of computers!

CONTENTS

CHAPTER 3

Formatting your presentation   65

Introduction

Tomorrow you have two appointments: a visit to the dentist, and a presentation to an audience of strangers and friends.

Which one fills you with greater terror?

Whether it's to a group of potential customers, a national conference of fellow workers, or a local community group, delivering an address can be an intimidating prospect.

Faced with these situations, you'll want to learn about any tools that will help you to feel less pressurised and more organized – tools that will make you more confident and help you make your points more effectively. This is where presentation software comes in.

In this module, you will discover how to create support materials that will reinforce your message, both textually and graphically. You will also find out how to design your materials – both on-screen slides and paper handouts – so as to maximize their audience impact.

Software won't turn a bad presentation into a good one. But it can help a good presentation succeed in its aim: better communication of your bright ideas.

Think of this module as your chance to speak rather than be spoken to. Good luck with it.

CHAPTER 1

Presentation basics

In this chapter

Slides are the building blocks of a visual presentation. In this chapter you will learn how to use Microsoft PowerPoint to create simple slides, enter text in them, and save your work.

New skills

At the end of this chapter, you should be able to:
- Explain what presentation software is used for
- Start and quit PowerPoint
- Create and close a presentation
- Insert slides in an presentation
- Type, edit, and delete text in a slide
- Save a presentation to hard disk or diskette
- Use PowerPoint's online help facilities
- Modify PowerPoint's toolbar and menu display

New words

At the end of this chapter you should be able to explain the following terms:

- Presentation software
- Slide
- Title slide
- Placeholder
- AutoLayout
- Normal view

Presentations and presentation software

When you demonstrate a new product, describe the results of your research, or announce a new organizational structure, you typically make a speech. Two things can help your speech to have a greater impact:

- **Visual Aids**: To grab your audience's attention, and reinforce your messages, you could show them a variety of visual aids while you are talking.

- **Handouts**: To ensure that your audience retains key information, you could give them handouts to take away and study afterwards.

How do you create your visual aids? You have four main options:

- **OHP foils**: You could print out your visual aids on transparent plastic sheets (known as foils or acetates), and display them using an overhead projector (OHP).

- **35mm slides**: You could create 35mm slides, similar to photographic slides, and display them with a slide projector.

- **Computer screen:** For presentations to individuals or small groups you could show your presentation on the screen of a portable computer.

- **Digital projector**: You could connect your desktop or portable computer to a digital projector, and display your presentation on a large screen or even a suitable wall.

The choice of output depends on the number of people in your audience, the size of the room in which you are making the presentation, the technology available – and your budget.

Your visual aids should reinforce and complement what you say – they shouldn't *duplicate* it. Text should be kept to a minimum, using headlines and bullet points. Where possible, include images (pictures, graphs, charts, maps, cartoons, diagrams).

Presentation software such as Microsoft PowerPoint can help you to design and produce the visual aids and the printed handouts. Unfortunately, it doesn't help you with the speech. For the ECDL, you need to know how to produce the visual aids and handouts; you don't have to make a speech. Phew!

Presentation software

Applications such as Microsoft PowerPoint that create visual aids and printed handouts for use when addressing an audience.

Whatever your type of presentation, it will consist of a series of individual slides.

Slide

> *The basic building block of a visual presentation. It is
> equivalent to a page in a printed document. A slide
> typically contains text and graphics, and possibly sound,
> animations, and video.*

Now that you know the purpose of presentation software,
you are ready to create your first slides.

Starting PowerPoint

Double-click on the PowerPoint icon.

PowerPoint

–or–

Choose **Start | Programs | PowerPoint**.

PowerPoint does not create a new, blank presentation when
you start the application. Instead it shows a dialog box that offers
a number of options. Your two main options are as follows.

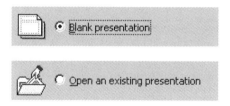

You need not select any of the presentation options on this
initial dialog box. You can just click **Cancel**. (This closes the
dialog box – it does not close PowerPoint!) You can then work
with PowerPoint's pull-down menus and toolbar buttons to
create a new presentation or edit an existing one.

Creating a presentation

In this first exercise you will create a slide called the title slide. The first slide in any PowerPoint presentation is always the title slide. It introduces your presentation to the audience. Like the first page of a book, it usually has a different layout from the rest of the presentation.

Title slide
> *The first slide in a presentation. Typically, it has a different layout from the rest of the presentation.*

Exercise 1.1: Creating the title slide of a presentation

1 How you create a presentation depends on whether or not PowerPoint is already open on your PC:

File New button

- If PowerPoint is not already open, open it now. On the initial dialog box displayed, click Blank Presentation and then click **OK**.

- If PowerPoint is already open, click the File New button on the Standard toolbar.

2 PowerPoint displays a dialog box offering you a choice of ready-made layouts (called AutoLayouts) for your slide. As you click on a layout, PowerPoint shows its name in an area at the right of the dialog box.

Click the first AutoLayout, which PowerPoint calls Title Slide, and then click **OK**.
(Alternatively, double-click on the Title Slide AutoLayout.)

3   You are now shown a screen that contains two boxes surrounded by dotted lines. PowerPoint calls these boxes placeholders.

Click anywhere in the top placeholder.

4   The border of the placeholder changes and a blinking text cursor appears inside it. You can now type text in the placeholder.

Type the following text in the top placeholder:

Product Launch

5   Click in the lower placeholder and type the following text:

Round Wheels

Your screen should now look as shown below.

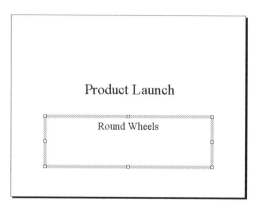

Congratulations! You have created the first slide of your first presentation in PowerPoint. You have also met two important terms in PowerPoint: *placeholder* and *AutoLayout.*

Placeholder

A frame or box within a slide for holding text or graphics.

Remember:

- Click on a placeholder to select it so that you can type or edit text.

- Click anywhere outside a placeholder to deselect it.

AutoLayout

One of 24 ready-made slide layouts. They typically include placeholders for text and other objects, such as images and charts.

Adding slides to your presentation

After the title slide, you will want to create further slides to hold the main body of your presentation. Exercise 1.2 shows you how.

Exercise 1.2: Adding a second slide

1   Choose **Insert | New Slide** or click the Insert New Slide button on the Standard toolbar.

2   Select the AutoLayout that you want to use. This time, select the Bulleted List, and then click **OK**.

Insert New Slide button

3 Click in the top placeholder
   and type:

   Amazing Features

4 Click in the lower placeholder, type the following, and
   press Enter:

   Smooth Travelling for Passenger Comfort

   Notice that PowerPoint places a bullet character (•) in
   front of your line of text.

5 Type the following and press Enter:

   Reduced Fuel Consumption

6 Continue typing lines of text and pressing Enter until
   your second slide looks as shown.

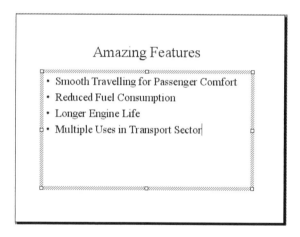

(Do not press Enter after your final line of text. If you do,
PowerPoint displays another line beginning with a
bullet. You can delete such an unnecessary line and
bullet by pressing the Backspace key twice.)

Well done! That's two slides created already.

Editing your text

If you make a typing error in PowerPoint, you can quickly correct your mistake using either of the following two keys:

- **Backspace**: Deletes the character to the *left* of the cursor. You will find the Backspace key at the top-right of the keyboard, just above the Enter key.

- **Delete:** Deletes the character to the *right* of the cursor. You will find the Delete key in a group of six keys to the right of the Enter key.

Moving between slides

When you have more than a single slide in your presentation, you will want to be able to view and work with each particular one:

- Press the Page Down key to move forward, one slide at a time.

- Press the Page Up key to move backwards through your presentation, one slide at a time.

- Press Home to go to the very first slide.

- Press End to go to the last slide.

On a desktop PC, you will find these four keys in a group of six keys to the right of the Enter key.

In the next exercise, you will add a third slide after the second one.

Exercise 1.3: Adding a third slide

1 Is your second slide currently displayed? If not, press Page Down to view it.

2 Choose **Insert | New Slide** or click the New Slide button on the Standard toolbar.

Insert New Slide button

3 Select the AutoLayout named 2 Column Text and click **OK**. Your screen should look as shown.

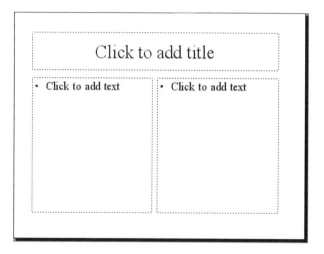

4 Click in the top placeholder and type the following:

Choice of Colours

5 Click in the left placeholder, type the following two lines of text, pressing Enter after the first line only:

Red

Green

6 Click in the right placeholder, type the following two lines of text, pressing Enter after the first line only:

Blue

Grey

Your slide should look as shown.

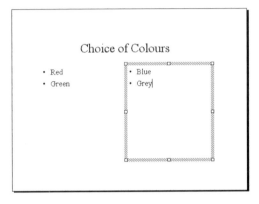

You have now created a three-slide presentation.

Location of inserted slides

PowerPoint always inserts a new slide *after* the slide that is displayed when you choose the **Insert | New Slide** command or click the Insert New Slide button on the Standard toolbar.

New slide at end of presentation

To insert a new slide *at the end* of your presentation (as in Exercises 1.2 and 1.3):

- Display the final slide

- Insert the new slide.

New slide within presentation

To insert a new slide anywhere *within* your presentation:

* Display the slide that will be located *before* your new slide

* Insert the new slide.

Saving your presentation

Although your presentation contains only three slides, you should save it now. As with other applications, the first time that you save a file in PowerPoint you are asked to specify:

* The location on your PC where you want your file saved

* The name of your new file.

PowerPoint file name extension

The file names of PowerPoint presentations end in .ppt. This helps you to distinguish PowerPoint files from other file types, such as Word (.doc) or Excel (.xls).

Exercise 1.4: Saving and naming your presentation

1 Choose **File | Save** or click the Save File button on the Standard toolbar.

Save File button

2 The first time that you save a presentation, PowerPoint prompts you to select a location. By default, PowerPoint suggests that you save your presentations in the My Documents folder. Accept or amend this location, as required.

3 PowerPoint prompts you to give a name to your new file. Type a name that you will find easy to remember and recognize. If your initials are KB, for example, call it KBpres1.

You need not type '.ppt' after your file name when saving a file. PowerPoint adds the three-letter file name extension automatically.

4 Click the Save button to save the file and close the dialog box.

Saving to a diskette

In the next exercise you will save your presentation again, this time on a floppy diskette.

Exercise 1.5: Saving your presentation to a diskette

1 Insert a diskette in the diskette drive of your computer:

- If it is a new diskette, ensure that it is formatted.

- If it is a previously used one, ensure that there is sufficient space on it to hold the presentation file. Your file should be about 12KB in size.

2 Choose **File | Save As** and locate the A: drive.

3 PowerPoint suggests the current file name (for example, KBpres1.ppt) for you to accept or amend. Click Save to save the file and close the dialog box.

4 When finished, use **File | Save As** again to resave the file to its original location on your computer. (You will be asked if you want to replace the original file: click **OK**.)

If you do not resave your presentation at its original location, saving the file in future (by clicking the Save button on the Standard toolbar or choosing **File | Save**) will save the presentation to the diskette and not to your computer's hard disk.

PowerPoint presentation

A file containing one or more slides. Presentation files end in .ppt.

Undo and Redo

Enter the wrong text? Press a wrong key? Don't panic. PowerPoint allows you to undo your most recent text entry or editing action if it has produced unwanted results. To undo an action:

- Choose **Edit | Undo**.

  –or–

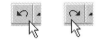

Undo and Redo buttons

- Click the Undo button on the Standard toolbar. Pressing Undo repeatedly reverses your last series of actions.

To view a list of recent actions that you can undo, click the arrow at the right of the Undo button. If you undo an action and then change your mind, click the Redo button (to the right of the Undo button).

   Practise using the Undo and Redo options by deleting characters from the text on your slides, and then reversing your deletions.

Views of your presentation

PowerPoint enables you to look at your presentation in four main ways or 'views': normal view, slide sorter view, notes view and Slideshow view. Let's look in detail at normal view. You will learn about the other three views in Chapters 2 and 3.

Working in Normal view

This is the default view. It's the view you have been using in this chapter. Normal view contains three sub-windows or 'panes':

- **Slide pane**: This is where you work on a *single slide* – you can add and amend text, graphics and multimedia elements.

- **Outline pane**: Here you can work with the text of *all slides* in your presentation in a structured way. You will learn more about outlines in Chapter 2.

- **Notes pane**: This lets you add and edit speaker notes. You will learn more about speaker notes in Chapter 3.

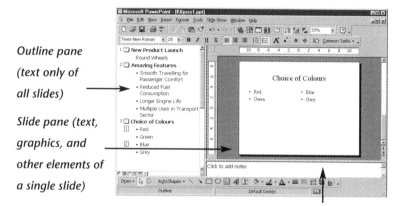

Outline pane (text only of all slides)

Slide pane (text, graphics, and other elements of a single slide)

Notes pane (additional text for presenter)

Changing the pane size

You can adjust the size of the different panes by clicking on and then dragging the pane borders. Try it and see!

- Move your cursor over a pane border. Notice how the cursor changes shape.

- Hold down the left mouse button, and move the mouse in any direction.

- Finally, release the mouse button.

You can reverse your pane resizing action by dragging the pane border back to its original location.

Normal view

A PowerPoint view composed of a Slide pane (where you work with one slide at a time), an Outline pane (where you see work with the text of all slides) and a Notes pane (where you can work with additional text for the presenter).

Zoom views

PowerPoint's Zoom feature enables you to magnify or reduce the screen display. You can use Zoom in either of two ways:

- Click in the zoom box on the Standard toolbar, enter a number between 10% and 400%, and press Enter.

- Choose **View | Zoom**, and select a magnification or reduction from the Zoom dialog box.

75%
400%
300%
200%
150%
100%
75%
66%
50%
33%
25%
Fit

When in normal view, your magnification or reduction affects *only* the pane in which the cursor is located.

Zoom and printing

The Zoom feature affects only the way that PowerPoint displays a presentation on-screen – and *not* how a presentation is printed. (You will learn about printing presentations in Chapter 2.)

PowerPoint's toolbars

PowerPoint's toolbars give you convenient, one-click access to the commands that you use most often. By default, PowerPoint displays just three toolbars:

- The Standard and Formatting toolbars, located on a single row, across the top of the screen.

- The Drawing toolbar, located along the bottom of the screen. You will learn more about the Drawing toolbar in Chapter 4.

PowerPoint's Drawing toolbar

Standard and Formatting toolbars

The toolbar buttons that you will need most frequently are located on just two toolbars – the Standard and the Formatting toolbars. By default, PowerPoint displays both on a *single* line.

To display them as two, individual toolbars at the top of your screen, follow these steps:

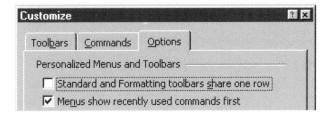

- Choose **Tools | Customize** and click the **Options** tab.

- Deselect the Standard and Formatting toolbars share one row checkbox, and choose **Close**.

PowerPoint's Standard toolbar

File | File | Insert
New | Save | New Slide

The Standard toolbar includes buttons for managing files – that is, PowerPoint presentations – and for inserting new slides. You have already used three of these buttons (File New, File Save, and Insert New Slide) in this chapter.

   The Formatting toolbar includes buttons for changing the appearance and position of text, and for working with bullets.

PowerPoint's Formatting toolbar

Rather than introduce all these buttons at once, we will explain each one as it becomes relevant through this ECDL Presentations module.

Hiding and displaying toolbars

You can display or hide any of PowerPoint's toolbars, according to your personal preference.

- To display a particular toolbar, choose **View | Toolbars** and select the toolbar that you want to display. On the toolbar sub-menu, PowerPoint displays a check mark against the toolbar(s) that you have selected.

- To hide a particular toolbar, choose **View | Toolbars** and select the toolbar that you want to hide. On the toolbar sub-menu, PowerPoint removes the check mark from the toolbar.

The check marks beside the Standard and Formatting toolbars indicate that they are already selected for display on-screen.

Hiding and displaying toolbar buttons

You can remove one or more buttons from a toolbar. Follow these steps:

- Display the toolbar that you want to change.

- Hold down the Alt key, and drag the button off the toolbar.

- PowerPoint removes the selected button from the toolbar.

Want the button back again? Follow this procedure:

- Display the toolbar. Click on More Buttons (at the very end of the toolbar) and then on **Add or Remove Buttons**.

- Click the button you want to display again.

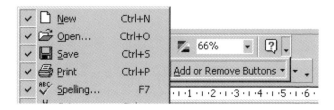

- Click anywhere outside the menu to close it.

PowerPoint redisplays the button on the toolbar.

PowerPoint's personalized menus

By default, when you first choose a menu, PowerPoint displays only *some* of the commands on that menu. To view a complete list, click the double-arrow at the bottom of the menu.

If you choose a command that is not displayed by default, PowerPoint adds it to the displayed list the next time that you choose the menu.

To view *all* commands each time you choose a menu, follow these steps:

- Choose **Tools | Customize** and click the **Options** tab.

- Deselect the Menus show recently used commands first option, and choose **Close**.

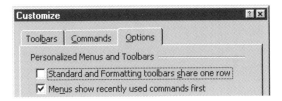

Online help

PowerPoint offers a searchable online help system. You can search through and read online help in two ways: from dialog boxes, or from the **Help** menu.

- The 'help' in online help means that the information is there to assist you understand and use the application.

- The 'online' means that the material is presented on the computer screen rather than as a traditional printed manual.

Using Help from dialog boxes

Exercise 1.6: Using online help in a dialog box

1 Choose **File | Print** to display the Print dialog box.

2 Click the question mark symbol near the top-right of the dialog box. PowerPoint displays a question mark to the right of the cursor.

3 Drag the mouse down and right, and click anywhere in the Name box.

4   PowerPoint now displays help text telling you about the selected box.

> Click a printer in the **Name** box. The information that
> appears below the **Name** box applies to the selected
> printer. The printer you click is the default printer for
> the rest of the current PowerPoint session, or until
> you change it.

Practise Exercise 1.6 with other dialog boxes in PowerPoint.

Using Help menu options

You can also access online help from the **Help** menu.

Contents tab	**Answer Wizard**	**Index tab**
This offers short descriptions of PowerPoint's main features.	*Type your question in the box at the top-left of the dialog box, and click **Search**.*	*Type the word phrase you are interested in and click **Search**.*
Where you see a heading with a book symbol, double-click it to view the related sub-headings.	*PowerPoint displays a list of suggested help topics in the lower-left.*	*PowerPoint displays all matches from the online help in the lower left of the dialog box.*
Double-click on a question mark symbol to read the online help text.	*Click on a topic to display the associated text in the right pane.*	*When you find the index entry that you are looking for, click on it to display the associated text in the right pane.*

Choose **Help | Microsoft PowerPoint Help** or click the Online Help button on the Standard toolbar to display the three-tabs online help dialog box.

As you search through and read online help topics, you will see the following buttons at the top of the online help window:

- **Hide/Show**: Hides or displays the left pane of the online help dialog box.

- **Back/Forward**: Moves you backwards and forwards through previously visited help topics.

- **Print**: Prints the currently displayed help topic.

- **Options**: Offers a number of display choices.

Take a few minutes to look through PowerPoint's online help system. Remember that you are free to use online help during an ECDL test.

Closing a presentation

To close a PowerPoint presentation:

- Choose File | Close

  –or–

- Click the Close button on the presentation window.

If you have made changes to your presentation since you last saved it, PowerPoint prompts you to save the changes before it closes the file.

Close PowerPoint
Close Presentation

Quitting PowerPoint

To close PowerPoint:

- Choose **File** | **Exit**

    –or–

- Click the Close button on the PowerPoint window.

If you have left open any presentations containing unsaved work, PowerPoint prompts you to save them.

You can close your presentation and PowerPoint. You have now completed Chapter 1 of the ECDL *Presentations* module.

Chapter summary: so now you know

A *presentation* is an address to an audience, accompanied by visual aids, such overhead projection foils (OHPs), and possibly handouts for the audience. *Presentation software*, such as PowerPoint, helps you prepare visual aids and printed handouts. PowerPoint file names end in *.ppt*.

The basic building blocks of a presentation are called *slides*. When you create a new presentation, PowerPoint automatically creates a single new slide. You insert further slides individually. PowerPoint always inserts a new slide *after* the one currently displayed.

When you create a new slide, you can choose from 24 ready-made slide layouts called *AutoLayouts*. One layout, called the Title layout, is designed for the first or *title slide* of a presentation. Each slide layout contains one or more boxes called *placeholders*, within which you type and edit.

PowerPoint offers a number of *views* – ways of looking at your slides. In the default normal view, the screen is split into three panes: a *Slide pane* (where you work with one slide at a time), an *Outline pane* (where you work with the text of all slides) and a *Notes pane* (where you can work with additional text for the presenter). You can adjust the size of the different panes by clicking on and then dragging the pane borders.

You can move forward and backward through a presentation, one slide at a time, by pressing the Page Down and Page Up keys. Press Home to go to the very first slide, and End to go to the last slide.

You can modify the toolbar display so that the features you use most often are readily available.

PowerPoint includes a built-in help facility that contains reference material on all the software's functions, and many helpful tips for creating convincing presentations.

CHAPTER 2

Working with bullet points

In this chapter

In Chapter 1 you learnt how to create a presentation by inserting a series of individual slides and typing text on each one. Now you will discover a second method: entering the text of all slides in the Outline pane, so avoiding the need to switch forward and backward through individual slides.

Also in this chapter you will learn about Slide Sorter view, which enables you to display all slides in a presentation at once and to check that the appearance of slides is consistent.

You can use the Outline pane and Slide Sorter view for changing the order of the slides in your presentation, and for copying slides within and between presentations.

New skills

At the end of this chapter you should be able to:
- Open a saved presentation
- Promote or demote the level of a bullet point
- Increase or decrease the spacing between bullet points
- Copy or cut and paste text within a slide or presentation, and between presentations
- Copy slides within and between presentations
- Import text from Microsoft Word or another non-PowerPoint source
- Change the bullet character
- Apply and change numbered bullets
- Run a PowerPoint presentation on your computer
- Hide and unhide individual slides

New words

At the end of this chapter you should be able to explain the following terms:
- Bullet point
- Outline pane
- Slide Sorter view

Opening a presentation

In this chapter you will work with the three-slide presentation that you created in Chapter 1. You begin by opening your saved presentation.

Exercise 2.1: Opening a presentation

1   How you open a saved presentation depends on whether or not PowerPoint is already open on your PC:

    *   If PowerPoint is not already open, open it now. On the initial dialog box displayed, click the Open an existing presentation option. Go to Step 2.

    *   If PowerPoint is already open, choose **File | Open** or click the File Open button on the Standard toolbar.

File Open button

2   Locate and select the three-slide presentation that you saved in Chapter 1, and click **OK**. Your presentation now opens on the screen.

Different levels of bullet points

Except for the title slide, the text on PowerPoint slides typically consists of *bullet points* – a bullet character such as a filled circle (•) or square (■) followed by one or a few words of text.

Different bullet points may contain different categories or 'levels' of information. Consider the following two sample slides.

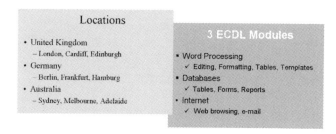

Each slide has two levels of bullet points: three *main* bullet points, each of which contains three *minor* points. The two different levels of bullet points are distinguished by:

- Different indents (the distance from the left edge of the slide)

- Different font sizes (the minor bullet points are in smaller text)

- Different bullet characters.

PowerPoint enables you to change bullet point levels with a single mouse click; it alters the indents, font size and bullet characters for you. Follow Exercise 2.2 to discover how.

Bullet point

A bullet character (such • or ■) followed by one or a few words of text. Bullet points may be at different levels, indicated by their indention, bullet character, and font size.

Exercise 2.2: Promoting and demoting bullets

1 Use the Page Down or Page Up keys to display the second slide of your presentation.

2 Click at the end of the fourth bullet point.

Amazing Features

- Smooth Travelling for Passenger Comfort
- Reduced Fuel Consumption
- Longer Engine Life
- Multiple Uses in Transport Sector

Click here

3 Press Enter to begin a new bullet point.

4 Type the following three words, pressing Enter after the first and second words only:

Cars

Bicycles

Trucks

Your new bullet points should look as shown.

- Multiple Uses in Transport Sector
- Cars
- Bicycles
- Trucks

5 Click at the start of the word 'Car'. Then drag down and to the right with the mouse until you have selected all three new bullet points.

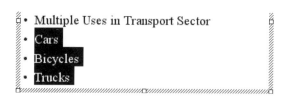

6 Click the Demote button on the Formatting toolbar. Notice how PowerPoint changes the display of the selected bullets points.

Click anywhere else on the slide to deselect the three bullet points.

7 As practice, select the three bullet points again, click the Promote button, and view the effect on the bullet points. When finished, and with the bullet points selected, click on the Demote button. The bullet points are again demoted.

Promote button

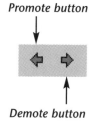

Demote button

The three demoted bullet points are variously known as minor bullets, sub-bullets, or level-two bullets. You are advised to avoid using more than two levels of bullets on a slide. Otherwise, you risk confusing your audience.

Changing the bullet character

By default, PowerPoint uses the filled black circle (•) and the dash (–) as the bullet characters for the first two levels of bullet points.

As Exercise 2.3 shows, you can choose from a range of other bullet character and colour options.

Exercise 2.3: Changing the bullet character

1 Display the second slide of your presentation, and select the first bullet point.

2 Choose **Format | Bullets and Numbering**. On the Bulleted tab of the dialog box, select the hollow circle bullet, and click **OK**.

Hollow Circle bullet

3 Select the second bullet point, choose **Format | Bullets and Numbering**, and, on the Bulleted tab, select the filled square bullet.

Filled Square bullet

Click on the arrow to the right of the Colour drop-down list and select the colour blue.

When finished, click **OK**.

4 Select the third bullet point, choose **Format | Bullets and Numbering**, and click in the **Picture** button.

You are now shown
PowerPoint's Picture
Bullet gallery.

Select a bullet by clicking on
it, and then click **OK** to close
the Picture Bullet gallery.

PowerPoint replaces the
default bullet character with
the bullet you selected from
its Picture Bullet gallery.

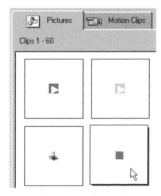

Picture Bullet gallery

5 Select the three minor bullet points on the slide, choose
   Format | Bullets and Numbering, and, on the Bulleted
   tab, click the **Character** button.

   In the Bullet dialog box, select Wingdings in the Bullets
   from: drop-down list, click on any displayed character to
   select it, and then click **OK**.

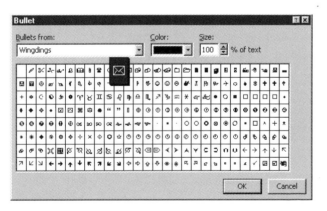

Your selected bullet character is now applied to the three minor bullet points.

6 The purpose of this exercise is not to change your slide but to show you the choices available for selecting bullet characters.

As the final step, press the Undo button repeatedly to return your slide to what it was at the beginning of this exercise.

Numbering bullet points

You can use sequentially increasing numbers (1, 2, 3, ...) or letters (a, b, c, ...) as bullet characters on your slides. Numbered lists are an appropriate choice when the order of reading is important, such as in directions and instructions.

To apply a numbered list to selected text:

Numbering button

• Click the Numbering button on the formatting toolbar.

–or–

• Choose **Format | Bullets and Numbering**, click the Numbered tab, select your numbering option, and click **OK**.

You can accept or change the default colour and starting value of the number or letter, and its size relative to the text of the line.

Exercise 2.4: Creating a slide with numbered bullets

1   You are about to add a fourth slide at the end of your presentation. So display your third slide, entitled 'Choice of Colours', and click the Insert New Slide button on the standard toolbar.

Insert New Slide button

2   Select the Bulleted List AutoLayout, click **OK**, and type the following text in the top placeholder of your new slide:

Marketing Plan

3   In the lower placeholder of your new slide, type the following bullet points:

Develop pricing plan
Build distribution network
National launch
International launch

4   Select the four bullet points that you typed in Step 3, and click the Numbering button on the Formatting toolbar.

PowerPoint applies its default numbering style to your bullet points.

1. Develop pricing plan
2. Build distribution network
3. National launch
4. International launch

In the next exercise you will change the numbering style.

Exercise 2.5: Changing the numbering style

1   Display your fourth slide, select the four numbered bullet points, and choose **Format | Bullets and Numbering**.

2   On the dialog box displayed, change the Size % of text to 120, the Colour to green, and the Start at value to 2. Click **OK**.

3   Notice the effect on your slide. Use the Undo option to return your slide to what it was at the beginning of this exercise.

Line spacing

On some slides you may have very few lines of text. On others, you may have quite a lot. PowerPoint allows you to 'space out' or 'squeeze' lines of text so that they fit the area of a single slide. Exercise 2.6 provides an example.

Exercise 2.6: Changing the line spacing

1   Display the third slide of your presentation.

2   Select the two bullet points in the left placeholder.

3   Choose **Format | Line Spacing**, change the Line spacing value from 1 to 2 Lines and click **OK**.

4 Repeat Steps 2 and 3 for the two bullet points in the right placeholder.

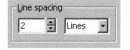

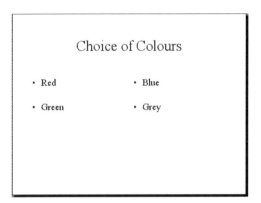

Your slide should now look as shown.

Save your presentation.

The **Format | Line Spacing** dialog box also allows you to alter the spacing before and after one or more selected lines.

Text alignment

Alignment refers to the *position* of text on a slide. Each of the three common options (left-, right- and centre-aligned) can be applied by clicking the associated button on the Formatting toolbar or by choosing the **Format | Alignment**.

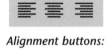

Alignment buttons:
Left, Centre and Right

By default, PowerPoint applies the following text alignment to slides:

- **Title slide**: All text is centre-aligned.

- **Other slides**: Title text is centred; bullet points are left-aligned.

As with other Microsoft Office applications, aligning text in PowerPoint is a two-step process: first select, then align. Exercise 2.7 shows you how.

Exercise 2.7: Changing text alignment

1 Display your second slide and select all the bullets points in the lower placeholder.

2 Choose **Format | Alignment | Centre** or click the Centre-align button on the Formatting toolbar.

Amazing Features

- Smooth Travelling for Passenger Comfort
  - Reduced Fuel Consumption
    - Longer Engine Life
- Multiple Uses in Transport Sector
  – Cars
  – Bicycles
  – Trucks

Click anywhere else to deselect the bullet points.

Your slide should look as shown.

3 Your slide was easier to read before you centre-aligned the text. Select all the bullet points again, and click the Left-align button on the Formatting toolbar. Your slide should look as it was at the start of this exercise. Save your presentation.

A fourth alignment option of justified text is available only with the **Format | Alignment** command and not on the Formatting toolbar. Avoid justifying text on slides: it can be difficult for your audience to read.

About outlines

In PowerPoint, an outline is the text of all slides in a presentation, with the text positioned in such a way that you can identify:

- Text that is the *title* of a slide

- Text that is a *bullet point* within a slide.

Consider the following presentation about ECDL, written as an outline:

> Overview
> Benefits for Schools
> > Computer literacy for pupils
> > Modular, practical syllabus
> > Not tied to one IT supplier
> Benefits for Colleges
> Benefits for Training Providers
> Benefits for Employers
> > Skills benchmark for new employees
> > Measure of user competence throughout organization
> > Reduction in IT support costs

As you can see, there are five slide titles. Of these, only slide two (Benefits for Schools) and slide five (Benefits for Employers) currently contain bullet points. Notice that the text of bullet points is indented further than the text of the slide titles. (The term indented means 'moved in from the left margin'.)

Working in the Outline pane

The Outline pane in Normal view enables you to enter and edit text throughout your presentation without the need to switch forward and backward through individual slides. You can also use the Outline pane to change the levels of text, and to change the order of the slides.

Outline Pane

In Normal view, this shows the text of all your slides, so that you can judge how well your ideas and text flow from one slide to the next.

In Exercise 2.8 you will create a new presentation, and type and structure its text in the Outline pane.

Exercise 2.8: Creating a presentation in the Outline pane

1 Click the File New button on the Standard toolbar.

2 On the New Slide dialog box, select the AutoLayout named Title Slide, and click **OK**.

File New button

3 Increase the size of the Outline pane in either of the following two ways:

- Using the mouse, click on the Outline pane border and drag it to the right.

Outline pane button

- Click the Outline pane button at the lower-left of your screen.

Your PowerPoint screen should look like that shown.

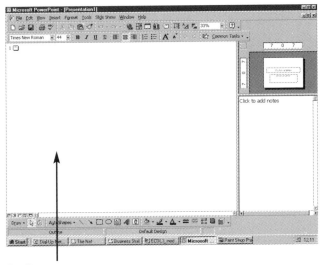

Outline pane

4 Click anywhere in the Outline pane to select the pane. Type the following two lines, pressing Enter after the first line only:

Promote button

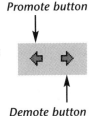

Demote button

ECDL: An Overview

ABC Training Corporation

Your text should look as shown.

Notice that the second line of text automatically takes on the attributes of the previous one: it appears as a slide title.

1 ☐ ECDL: An Overview
2 ☐ ABC Training Corporation|

5 Click anywhere in your second line of text, and then click the Demote button on the Formatting toolbar.

Your second line is now bullet point text within the first slide – and not a slide title.

1 ☐ **ECDL: An Overview**
     ABC Training Corporation

6 Press Enter at the end of your second text line and type the following four lines, pressing Enter after the first three:

Benefits for Schools
Benefits for Colleges
Benefits for Training Providers
Benefits for Employers

Your typed text should look as shown.

1 ☐ **ECDL: An Overview**
        ABC Training Corporation
        Benefits for Schools
        Benefits for Colleges
        Benefits for Training Providers
        Benefits for Employers|

7 Select the four lines that you have just typed, and click the Promote button on the Formatting toolbar. PowerPoint changes the

1 ☐ **ECDL: An Overview**
        ABC Training Corporation
2 ☐ **Benefits for Schools**
3 ☐ **Benefits for Colleges**
4 ☐ **Benefits for Training Providers**
5 ☐ **Benefits for Employers**

level of the selected lines so that they are now slide titles.

8 Click at the end of the line that contains the title of slide 2, 'Benefits for Schools', press Enter, click the Demote button, and type the following lines of text:

Computer literacy for pupils
Modular, practical syllabus
Not tied to one IT supplier

9 Click at the end of the line that contains the title of slide 3, 'Benefits for Colleges', press Enter, click the Demote button, and type the following lines of text:

Increased staff efficiency
Students better able to use IT facilities
Internationally recognized qualification

10 Click at the end of the line that contains the title of slide 4, 'Benefits for Training Providers', press Enter, click the Demote button, and type the following lines of text:

Capacity to offer valued qualification
Easy-to-deliver syllabus
Option to offer walk-in tests

11 Click at the end of the line that contains the title of slide 5, 'Benefits for Employers', press Enter, click the Demote button, and type the following lines of text:

Skills benchmark for new employees
Organisation-wide competence
Reduction in IT support costs

Your complete outline should now look as shown on the right.

12 Well done! You have created a second presentation.

Save your presentation. If your initials are KB, for example, name it KBpres2.ppt.

1 ▢ **ECDL: An Overview**
   ABC Training Corporation
2 ▢ **Benefits for Schools**
   • Computer literacy for pupils
   • Modular, practical syllabus
   • Not tied to one IT supplier
3 ▢ **Benefits for Colleges**
   • Increased staff efficiency
   • Students better able to use IT facilities
   • Internationally recognised qualification
4 ▢ **Benefits for Training Providers**
   • Capacity to offer valued qualification
   • Easy-to-deliver syllabus
   • Option to offer walk-in tests
5 ▢ **Benefits for Employers**
   • Skills benchmark for new employees
   • Organisation-wide competence
   • Reduction in IT support costs|

The outline and individual slides

What is the relationship between the outline text and the content of individual slides?

- **Slides**: PowerPoint creates a new slide for each slide title that you type in the Outline pane.

- **Bullet points**: PowerPoint inserts the demoted text lines in the Outline pane as bullet points on the associated slide.

Any text change you make in the Outline pane affects the individual slide, and any text change to a slide affects the Outline pane.

Switching between presentations

You now have two presentation files open at the same time in PowerPoint. To switch between open presentations:

- Click the **Window** menu, and then choose the file you want to work with.

  –or–

- Click the file name on the Windows taskbar.

Slide Sorter view

When you have more than one slide in your presentation, you will want to display different slides at different times on your screen. You have two main options:

- Press the Page Down or Page Up keys to move forward or backward through your presentation, one slide at a time.

- Switch to Slide Sorter view to display all your slides at once, and then double-click on the slide that you want to display.

To display your presentation in Slide Sorter view, choose the **View | Slide Sorter** command. You can return from Slide Sorter view to Normal view by choosing **View | Normal**.

Another way of switching between views is to click on the small buttons at the lower-left of your PowerPoint screen.

Slide Sorter view is also useful for:

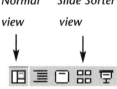

Normal   Slide Sorter
view   view

- Checking that the appearance of slides is consistent

- Changing the order of the slides in your presentation

- Copying slides within and between presentations.

Slide Sorter view

A view where you can see all slides of a presentation at once.

Switch to your first presentation and display it in Slide Sorter view. It should look as shown.

Your first presentation in Slide Sorter view

To see the result of the outline that you typed in Exercise 2.8, switch to your second presentation, and display it in Slide Sorter view. It should look as shown.

Your second presentation in Slide Sorter view

Slide Sorter view and zoom

You can use PowerPoint's Zoom feature to reduce or enlarge the display of Slide Sorter view. The default is 66%, allowing up to four slides to be displayed on a single row.

To display the five slides of your second presentation on a single row, reduce the Zoom value to 50% or less.

Reordering slides in Slide Sorter view

When you look at your slides in Slide Sorter view, you may decide to change the order in which they appear. You can do this in two ways:

- By dragging them with the mouse (better for small presentations)

- By using cut-and-paste (better for larger presentations).

Reordering by dragging

Follow these steps:

- In Slide Sorter view, click on the slide you want to move to select it. Notice that PowerPoint displays a thicker border around your selected slide.

- Drag it with the mouse so that a vertical line appears to the left of where you want to position the slide.

- Release the mouse button.

Reordering by cut and paste

You can cut, copy, and paste slides in PowerPoint as you would text in a word processor. Follow these steps:

- In Slide Sorter view, click the slide to select it.

- Choose **Edit | Cut** or click the Cut button on the Standard toolbar.

- Click on another slide to select it.

- Choose **Edit | Paste** or click the Paste button on the Standard toolbar.

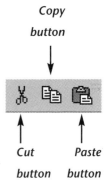

*Copy
button*

*Cut
button*

*Paste
button*

The pasted slide appears *after* (to the right or beneath) the slide you selected before you performed the paste action.

In Slide Sorter view, practise reordering the five slides in your presentation by dragging them to a new location, and then cut-and-pasting them back to their original locations.

Keyboard shortcuts

A fast way to perform copy, cut, and paste actions is to use the relevant shortcut keys. To copy a selected item, for example, hold down the Ctrl key and press the letter 'c' key.

Action	Keyboard Shortcut
Copy	CTRL + c
Cut	CTRL + x
Paste	CTRL + v

Copying and moving slides

You can copy and move slides within a presentation, and between different presentations. Exercises 2.9 and 2.10 provide examples.

Exercise 2.9 Copying a slide within a presentation

1 Display your second presentation, entitled 'ECDL: An Overview'. In Slide Sorter view, click on your title (first) slide to select it.

2 Press Ctrl+c to copy your title slide.

3 Click on your fifth slide to select it.

4 Press Ctrl+v to paste the title slide at the end of your presentation.

Your presentation now has six slides. In the final step, you will delete the slide that you pasted in Step 4.

5 With the pasted slide selected, press the Delete key.

Exercise 2.10: Copying a slide between presentations

1 Display your second presentation in Slide Sorter view.

2 Click the title slide, and press Ctrl+c.

3 Switch to your first presentation, entitled 'Product Launch', and display it in Slide Sorter view.

4 Click the second slide, entitled 'Amazing Features', to select it.

5 Press Ctrl+v. PowerPoint pastes the slide as the new third slide of your 'Product Launch' presentation.

6 With the pasted slide selected, press the Delete key.

Copying and moving text

To copy or move text from one part of a slide to another, or between different slides of the same or different presentations:

- Select the text by clicking and dragging.

- Copy or cut the text.

- Position your cursor where you want the text to appear.

- Paste the text.

Exercise 2.11 provides an example of cut-and-paste.

Exercise 2.11: Moving text within a slide

1 In Normal view, display the third slide of your first presentation, entitled 'Choice of Colours'.

2 Select the two bullet points in the right placeholder, and press Ctrl+x. The selected text is removed from the right placeholder.

3 Click in the left placeholder at the end of the second bullet point.

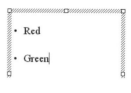

4 Press Enter. PowerPoint creates a new line beginning with a bullet character.

5 Press Ctrl+v to paste the two bullet points.

If PowerPoint adds an additional bullet character on a new line after the two bullet points that you pasted, press the Backspace key twice – once to remove the bullet character, and a second time to remove the new line.

6 Click anywhere in the right placeholder, and then click on its border. Press the Delete key to remove the right placeholder.

7 Choose **Format | Slide Layout** to display a list of AutoLayouts.

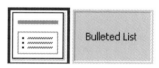

Click the option named Bulleted List, and then click Apply. Click on any bullet point.

Your third slide should now look as shown on the next page. Save your presentation.

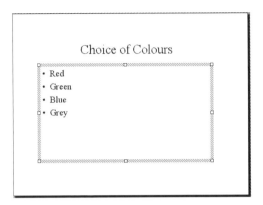

Importing text from another application

If you have text in another application, such as Microsoft Word, you can use that text in PowerPoint without having to retype it. The simplest way is as follows:

- In the other application, select the text.

- Copy it.

- In PowerPoint, position the cursor where you want the text to appear.

- Paste the text.

Follow the steps in Exercise 2.12 to discover how.

Exercise 2.12: Importing non-PowerPoint text

1   Display the second slide, entitled 'Amazing Features', of your first presentation. In Normal view, click the Insert New Slide button on the standard toolbar.

Insert New Slide button

The new slide becomes the third slide of your presentation; the former third and fourth slides are now your fourth and fifth slides.

2 Select the Bulleted List AutoLayout, and click **OK**.

3 Click in the top placeholder and type the text:

Online Help Text

4 Choose **Help | Microsoft PowerPoint Help**. If it is not already displayed, click the Contents tab.

5 Select the heading text in the right pane of the online help window, and press Ctrl+c to copy it.

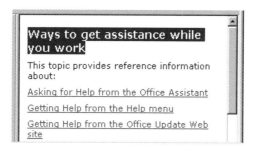

6 Switch back to PowerPoint. Ensure that the new slide that you created in Step 1 is displayed.

Click at the first bullet character, and press Ctrl+v to paste the selected text. Your slide should look as shown.

Online Help Text

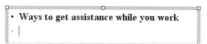

Notice how PowerPoint has created a second bullet character beneath your pasted text. PowerPoint assumes that you will want to add a second bullet point, either by typing it directly or by pasting it from another source.

7 Repeat Steps 5 and 6 for the following other headings from PowerPoint online help:

Asking for Help from the Office Assistant

Getting Help from the Help menu

Getting Help from the Office Update Web site

Asking for Help from the Office Assistant

When you have a question about a Microsoft Office program, you can ask the

Getting Help from the Help menu

Just click **Microsoft PowerPoint Help** on the **Help** menu. If the Assistant is turned

Getting Help from the Office Update Web site

You can connect to the Microsoft Office Update Web site and other Microsoft Web

Finding out what's new in PowerPoint 2000

Discover the new features in PowerPoint 2000 that make the product easier to use,

Finding out what's new in PowerPoint 2000

(Don't select from the list of hyperlinked headings near the top of the online help right-hand pane. Instead, select the headings as they appear down through the body of the text.)

After pasting the final bullet point, use the Backspace key twice to remove the bullet character and new line that PowerPoint automatically inserted beneath it.

8 The inserted text on your slide is in bold – as it was in online help.

B *I* <u>U</u> S

Bold button

Select the five bullet points and click the Bold button on the Formatting toolbar to remove the bold effect.

Your slide should look as shown overleaf. Save your presentation.

9 Close the Online Help window.

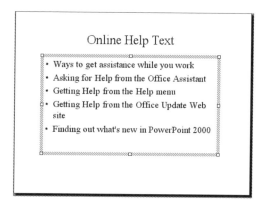

10 Display your presentation in Slide Sorter view. It should look as shown.

You can use the same method for copying to PowerPoint:

*   Text from a Word document

*   A cell, cell range, or chart from an Excel worksheet

*   A picture (such as a scanned photograph) from a graphics application.

Running your presentation

When you have created a number of slides, you can preview how they will look to your audience by choosing **View | Slide Show**. This will start the display at your first slide. To start the display at the current slide, click the Slide Show button at the bottom of the screen.

Your slides are shown without any PowerPoint menus, toolbars, or other screen elements that are displayed when you are creating or editing slides. To move between slides:

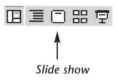

Slide show

- Press the Page Down, Page Up, Home, or End keys, as you would in Normal view.

  –or–

- Right-click anywhere on the screen with the mouse, and choose a navigation option from the pop-up menu displayed.

  –or–

- Click anywhere on the screen to move forward to the next slide.

To exit the slide show and return to your previous view, press the Esc key.

Slide Show view

> *A view you use for presenting your slides to your audience. PowerPoint's various menus and toolbars are not displayed in Slide Show view.*

Deleting and hiding slides

In Exercise 2.9 and 2.10, you deleted slides in Slide Sorter view by selecting them and then pressing the Delete key.

To delete a slide in Normal view, display the slide and choose **Edit | Delete Slide**.

Practise this command by deleting any of your slides. After deleting the slide, click the Undo button on the Standard toolbar to restore it to your presentation.

There may be times when you do not want to show a certain slide or slides in a presentation to a particular audience. PowerPoint allows you to 'hide' such slides, so that they remain part of your presentation but are not displayed.

To hide a slide:

- In Normal view, display the slide and choose **Slide Show | Hide Slide**.

- In Slide Sorter view, click the slide to select it before choosing the command.

To unhide a hidden slide, select it and choose **Slide Show | Hide Slide** again.

Practise this option by hiding a slide, running your presentation in Slide Show view, and then revealing the slide.

You can save and close your presentations, and close PowerPoint. You have now completed Chapter 2 of the ECDL *Presentations* module.

Chapter summary: so now you know

Except for the title slide, the text on PowerPoint slides typically consists of *bullet points* – a bullet character followed by one or a few words of text. *Bullet characters* can be symbols, sequentially increasing numbers (1, 2, 3, …) or letters (a, b, c, …).

Different bullet points may contain different categories or 'levels' of information. Different *bullet levels*, which are distinguished by different indents, font sizes, and bullet characters, may be *demoted* or *promoted*, as required.

The *Outline pane* of Normal view offers a fast way to enter and edit text, and to change the level of text and the order of slides.

PowerPoint's *Slide Sorter* allows you to display all slides in a presentation at once. It is useful for checking that the appearance of slides is consistent, changing the order of the slides in your presentation, and copying slides within and between presentations.

You can *copy-and-paste* text and other items from other applications into PowerPoint.

PowerPoint's *line spacing* feature allows you to 'space out' or 'squeeze' lines of text so that they fit the area of a single slide.

By default, PowerPoint centre-aligns text on title slides, and left-aligns text on all other slides. You can override these defaults on individual slides by using the *alignment* options.

You can preview how your slides will look to an audience in *Slide Show view*, which displays your slides without any PowerPoint menus, toolbars or other screen elements.

You can move between slides in Slide Show view by right-clicking anywhere on the screen with the mouse, and choosing a navigation option from the pop-up menu displayed. To exit Slide Show view and return to your previous view, press the Esc key.

PowerPoint allows you to *hide* one or more individual slides, so that they remain part of your presentation but are not displayed.

CHAPTER 3

Formatting your presentation

In this chapter

The presentations that you created in Chapters 1 and 2 contained black text against a plain white background. PowerPoint offers two main ways of formatting your slides to make them more attractive.

The first is to change the appearance of your presentation one slide at a time. The second is to reformat your entire presentation in a single action. The second, global approach is better: it saves you effort and time, and your slides benefit from having a consistent appearance.

New skills

At the end of this chapter, you should be able to:
- Apply text and background effects to individual slides
- Apply text and background effects to a presentation using the slide master

- Apply and customize a presentation colour scheme
- Prepare speaker notes
- Prepare handouts for your audience
- Print slides, handouts and speaker notes

New words

At the end of this chapter you should be able to explain the following terms:
- Slide master
- Colour scheme
- Handout

Presentation format

Slide formatting refers to the *appearance* of the slides in your presentation. It includes:

- **Text format**: The font, size and colour of text on slides, and any text effects such as bold, italics or shadows.

- **Background colour or pattern**: The solid (plain) colour or decorative pattern behind the text of your slides.

One way to format your slides is to change them one slide at a time. That is, display your first slide, reformat the text and background, and repeat this action for all slides in your presentation. Is there a faster way? Yes – in fact there are two.

Making global changes

PowerPoint offers two main methods of reformatting all slides in your presentation in a single operation:

- **Colour schemes**: These are combinations of text and background colours. You simply select the colour scheme you require, and PowerPoint applies it to all your slides. You can even change any of the built-in colour schemes to suit your needs or taste.

- **Slide master**: Every slide in a presentation is based on what PowerPoint calls a slide master. When you change the background or text format on the slide master, all slides on your presentation are updated accordingly.

(A third slide formatting option, called design templates, is explained in Chapter 6.)

What choices do I have?

As you experiment with PowerPoint's reformatting features, you may be overwhelmed by the number of options available. But really you have only three choices:

- **Dark text, light background**: In a lighted room, this is the preferred option.

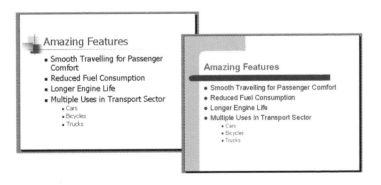

- **Light text, dark background**: In a darkened room, reversed type (text in a light colour, background in a dark colour) is easier for your audience to read.

Whichever choice you make, ensure that the colours you choose for text and background are sharply contrasting.

- **Solid or decorative background**: You are not limited to using a solid (single-colour) background in your slides. You can also specify gradients, textures, patterns, or pictures.

A word of caution: these decorative background options are intended to make your slides more exciting; however, if you do not use them carefully, they can make your slides illegible!

A plain slide that can be read easily is much more valuable (to you and your audience) than a fancy one that nobody can read.

Before working with colour schemes and the slide master, you need to be familiar with the text formatting options in PowerPoint.

Text format

Formatting refers to the *appearance* of text. It includes actions such as making text bolder (heavier), putting it in italics, or placing a shadow behind it. You may also change the text font, size, and colour.

You can apply text formatting by first selecting the text, choosing **Format | Font**, selecting your required options, and clicking **OK**.

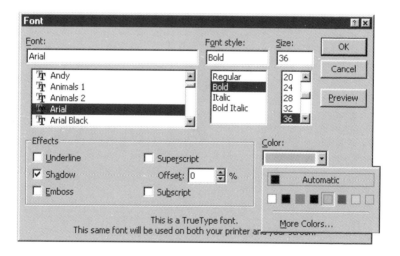

You can also apply most formatting to selected text by clicking the relevant buttons on the Formatting and Drawing toolbars.

Formatting toolbar

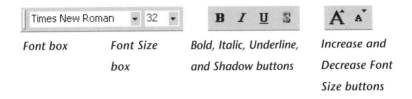

| Font box | Font Size box | Bold, Italic, Underline, and Shadow buttons | Increase and Decrease Font Size buttons |

Drawing toolbar

Font Color button

Let's look at PowerPoint's font options in more detail.

About fonts

You can see what fonts are installed on your computer by clicking the arrow on the drop-down Font box on the left of the Formatting toolbar. Most fonts fall into two categories (families):

- **Serif fonts**: So called because of their serifs (tails or squiggles). Common examples are Times New Roman and Garamond.

- **Sans serif fonts**: Common examples include Arial, Arial Narrow, and Gill. (Sans serif just means without serifs.)

In printed text, serif fonts are generally easier to read. For slides, however, sans serif fonts are a better choice.

Changing font

To change the font of selected text:

- Click the arrow to the right of the Font drop-down list box on the Formatting toolbar.

- Click the font you require from the list displayed.

Changing font on every slide

Want to replace the font on every slide? Just choose the **Format | Replace Fonts** command, select the current and replacement fonts, and click **Replace**.

Changing font case

You can change the case – for example, from lower- to upper-case – of a selected letter, word, or group of words using the options on the **Format | Change Case** command:

Your options are as follows:

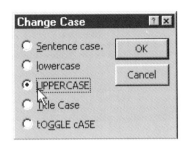

- **Sentence case**: Capitalizes the first letter of the first word in the selected sentence(s). All other letters in lower-case.

- **lower case**: Changes all text to lower-case.

- **UPPER CASE**: Changes all text to upper-case (capitals).

- **Title Case**: Makes the first letter of every word in the selected text upper-case. All other letters in lower-case.

- **tOGGLE cASE**: Changes the current case of all letters: upper-case becomes lower, and lower-case becomes upper.

Changing font size

Font size is measured in a non-metric unit called the point, with approximately 72 points equal to one inch.

To help you choose suitable font sizes, the placeholders in PowerPoint's AutoLayouts include built-in font size values.

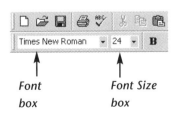

Font box   *Font Size box*

If you select the Bulleted List AutoLayout, for example, text you type in the top placeholder defaults to 44 points, and in the lower placeholder to 32 points. Fonts vary in their legibility, and you might need to choose a bigger point size for certain fonts.

Slide element	Default font size
Title Text	44 points
Main Bullet Points	32 points
Minor Bullet Points	28 points

To change the font size of selected text:

- Click the arrow to the right of the Font Size drop-down list box on the Formatting toolbar.

- Click the font size you require from the list displayed.

If your required value is not listed, you can type the font size directly in the box. Alternatively, you can increase or decrease font size, in four-point steps, by clicking the appropriate button on the Formatting toolbar.

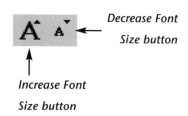

Decrease Font Size button

Increase Font Size button

Changing font colour

You can change the colour of selected text by clicking the arrow to the right of the Font Color button on the Drawing toolbar.

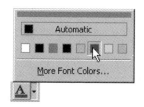

Don't see the colour you need? Click the **More Font Colors** button and select from the range available.

Changing font effects

You can apply bold, italics, underline, and shadow effects to selected text by clicking the relevant buttons on the Formatting toolbar.

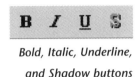

Bold, Italic, Underline, and Shadow buttons

Two font effects not available from any toolbar are superscript and subscript. To apply either effect to selected text, you need to display the **Format | Font** dialog box.

- **Superscript**: This raises the selected text above the other text on the same line, and reduces its font size. Superscript is used most commonly for mathematical notation.

  For example: 2^2, x^8, 10^3

- **Subscript**: The opposite of superscript. Subscript is text that is lowered beneath other text on the same line and is reduced in font size. Subscripts are commonly used in chemistry texts for formulas.

  For example: H_2SO_4

Exercise 3.1 demonstrates PowerPoint's text formatting options in action.

Exercise 3.1: Changing text format on a single slide

1 If PowerPoint is not already open, open it now.

Open your first presentation in Normal view. Display the second slide, entitled 'Amazing Features'.

Save your presentation before continuing further.

2 Select the slide title text. Using the Font box at the left of the Formatting toolbar, change the font to Arial.

3 With the title text still selected, click the Shadow button on the Formatting toolbar. PowerPoint applies a shadow effect to your slide title.

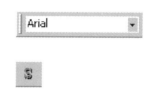

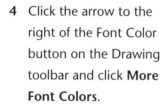

4 Click the arrow to the right of the Font Color button on the Drawing toolbar and click **More Font Colors**.

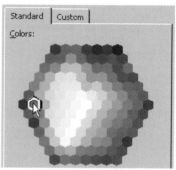

From the colours displayed, select a medium green, and click **OK**.

5 Select all the major and minor bullet points, change the font to Arial, and change the text colour to the medium green that you selected in Step 4 above.

Click anywhere else on the slide to deselect the text. Your slide should now look as shown.

Don't save your presentation yet.

You can imagine that, for a presentation containing a large number of slides, changing the font on each slide individually would take a lot of time and effort. In the next topic you will learn about the slide master, and use it to apply text effects to an entire presentation.

Working with the slide master

Whether you know it or not, every slide you insert in a PowerPoint presentation is based on a slide master.

- It is from the slide master that all slides take their default text formatting and positioning.

- Anything that you insert on the slide master appears automatically on every slide of your presentation.

As you will discover in Chapter 4, this is useful for company logos or for recurring graphics such as lines and borders.

To view the slide master, choose **View | Master | Slide Master**. It consists of two main placeholders:

- **Title placeholder**: Controls the format and positioning of text in every title placeholder in your presentation.

- **Object placeholder:** Controls the format and positioning of text in every non-title placeholder.

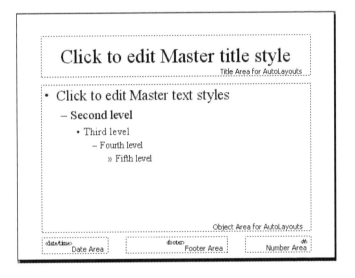

Along the bottom of the slide master you can see three footer placeholders – for the date/time, footer text, and slide numbering.

Your audience never sees the slide master; they see only its effects on the slides in your presentation. You can override the defaults supplied by the slide master on any individual slide.

Slide Master

This stores all the default attributes that you wish to apply to slides, including text formatting and positioning, background, and standard graphics, such as your company logo.

In the next exercise you will change the text format of your presentation by changing the slide master.

Exercise 3.2: Formatting text in the slide master

1   Choose **View | Master | Slide Master** and select the title text in the top placeholder.

2   Change its font to Arial, apply a Shadow effect, and change its colour to the medium green that you selected in Exercise 3.1.

3   Select the first and second level bullet points in the lower placeholder.

> • **Click to edit Master text styles**
>   – **Second level**

Change the font to Arial, and change the colour to medium green.

4   When finished, switch to Slide Sorter view. Notice that PowerPoint has reformatted the text of all your slides. Don't save your presentation yet.

Working with backgrounds

You can transform the appearance of your slides by changing their background. Follow Exercise 3.3 to discover how.

Exercise 3.3: Changing the background in the Slide Master

1 Choose **View | Master | Slide Master** to display your presentation's slide master.

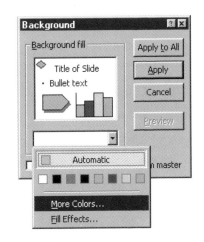

2 Choose **Format | Background**. Click on the drop-down list box, and select the **More Colors** option.

3 From the colours displayed, select a light yellow. Click **OK** and then **Apply to All**.

4 Choose **View | Slide Sorter** to verify that all slides in your presentation now have the yellow background.

5 How will your reformatted presentation appear to your audience? To find out, switch to Slide Show view and page through your slides.

6 Choose **File | Save As**, and save the presentation with a name that indicates its colour. If your initials are KB, for example, save it as KBpres1_green_on_yellow.ppt.

   In Slide Sorter view, your presentation should look as shown.

You now have two versions of your first presentation: one with black text against a white background, and a second with green text against a yellow background.

Slide master and backgrounds

You don't need to display your presentation's slide master in order to apply a background to all slides. When you choose **Format | Background**, the dialog box gives you two options: **Apply** (to this slide only) and **Apply to All** (the entire presentation). In the next exercise you will apply a decorative background to your presentation, and change the font to suit the new background.

Exercise 3.4: Applying a decorative background

1 In Normal view, choose **Format | Background**, click on the drop-down list near the bottom of the dialog box, and click **Fill Effects**.

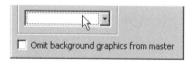

2 On the Gradient tab, select the Preset button. In the Preset colours drop-down list, select Daybreak. Click **OK** and then **Apply to All**.

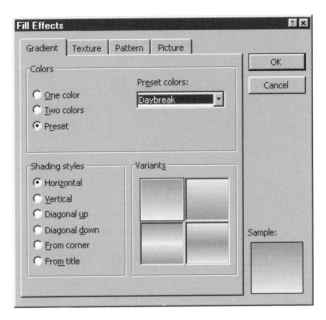

3   Choose **View | Master | Slide Master** to display your
    presentation's slide master.

4   In the top placeholder, select the title text. On the
    Drawing toolbar, click the arrow to the right of the Font
    Color button, click **More Font Colors**, select a darker
    shade of green, and click **OK**.

5   In the lower placeholder, select the first and second level
    bullet points. Change their font colour to the darker green.

    The darker green gives a better contrast against the
    background pattern, with the result that your slides are
    easier to read.

6   Switch to Slide Show view, and take look at how your
    presentation would appear to the audience.

    Notice that all the text on your second slide, entitled
    'Amazing Features', is still in the medium green that you
    applied to it in Exercise 3.1.

Why? Because, where a slide has been formatted individually, the slide master does not override the individual settings.

Display this second slide in Normal view, and change the colour of the slide title and bullet point text to the darker green. All your slides now have a common text colour.

7 When finished, choose **File | Save As**, and save the presentation with a name that indicates its background effect. If your initials are KB, for example, save it as KBpres1_daybreak.ppt.

In Slide Sorter view, your presentation should look as shown.

You now have three versions of your first presentation: black text with white background, green text with yellow background, and dark green with decorative 'daybreak' background.

Slide master and text options

You can use the slide master to change other attributes of text in your presentation in exactly the same way. In particular:

- **Bullet**, which allows you to choose the bullet character that applies to each level of text

- **Alignment**, which allows you to specify whether the text is to be aligned left or right, centred, or justified

- **Line Spacing**, which allows you to select the amount of space between lines in a paragraph and between different paragraphs

- **Case**, which allows you specify the case of slide titles or bullet points.

You can vertically align text in a placeholder, text box or object, then select the object type from the **Format** menu. In the dialog box that opens, go to the Text Box tab and select the required alignment in the text anchor point drop-down list. Click OK to apply the alignment.

Working with colour schemes

As you have seen, the slide master gives you total control over every aspect of your slides' text and background. Is there an even faster way to change your presentation's appearance?

Yes. PowerPoint comes supplied with a number of built-in colour schemes – professionally-designed combinations of background and text colours.

In Exercise 3.5 you will apply a preset colour scheme to a presentation. And in Exercise 3.6 you will learn how to customize a colour scheme.

Exercise 3.5: Applying a Colour Scheme

1   Open your second saved presentation, entitled 'ECDL: An Overview', and display it in Slide Sorter view.

In this view you will be better able to see how different colour schemes affect your presentation.

Save your presentation before continuing.

2   Choose **Format | Slide Color Scheme**. On the Standard tab, select the scheme with the yellow background, and click **Apply to All**.

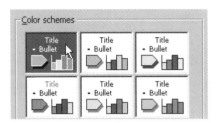

In Slide Sorter view, you can immediately see the impact on your presentation.

3   You already have one presentation with dark text against a light background. So choose **Format | Slide Color Scheme** again. This time select the blue background, and click **Apply to All**.

4   Choose **Format | Replace Fonts**. In the (replace) With: box, select the Arial font, and click **Replace**.

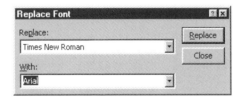

When finished, click **Close** to close the Replace Font dialog box. Do not save your presentation.

Customizing colour schemes

You don't have to accept the default options of PowerPoint's preset colour schemes. As the next exercise shows, you can customize a colour scheme to suit your taste or needs.

Exercise 3.6: Customizing a colour scheme

1 Choose **Format | Slide Color Scheme**. On the Custom tab, select Title text, and click the **Change Color** button.

2 From the colours displayed, select a medium green, and click **OK**.

3 On the Custom tab, select Text and lines, and click the **Change Color** button.

4 From the colours displayed, select a medium yellow, click **OK**, and then **Apply to All**.

5 Switch to Slide Show view and inspect your work.

6 When finished, choose **File | Save As**, and save the presentation with a name that indicates its colour scheme effect. If your initials are KB, for example, save it as KBpres2_yellow_on_blue.ppt.

In Slide Sorter view, your presentation should look as shown.

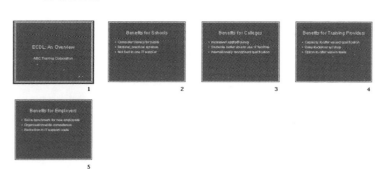

You now have two versions of your second presentation: one with black text on a white background, and a second with green titles and yellow bullet points on a blue background.

Colour scheme

A set of preset co-ordinated colours you can apply to your presentation to give it an attractive and consistent appearance.

Combining colour scheme and slide master effects

In any presentation, you are not faced with the choice of using the slide master *or* a colour scheme; you can use both when formatting the same presentation. For example, you could:

- Begin by selecting a preset colour scheme.

- Next customize some element(s) of the scheme.

- Then use the slide master to apply various effects – such as font sizes, line spacing, and special bullet characters – to your slides.

When all slides are not the same

Both the **Format | Background** and **Format | Slide Color Scheme** dialog boxes include an **Apply** (to current slide only) option. Typically, you use this option when:

- Your presentation deals with different topics, and the different sections would benefit from having different formatting.

- One or a few slides contain material that needs to stand out from the remainder of the presentation.

Even with the same colour scheme or background throughout a presentation, you can still emphasise particular slides by applying font effects to their text.

Speaker notes

For each slide that you create in a presentation, PowerPoint creates what it calls a speaker notes page. You can ignore or use these pages as you wish. Typically, you use speaker notes pages to remind you (or whoever is giving the presentation) of key points or background information.

You can enter or alter text in speaker notes pages at any stage when creating or editing your presentation.

Speaker notes

A page created by PowerPoint to accompany each slide. You can use it to record key points or additional details about your presentation.

Notes Page view

You can access a speaker notes page in either of two ways:

- In Normal view, you can type or edit text in the Notes pane at the lower right of your screen.

  If required, you can enlarge the Notes pane by dragging its pane borders upwards or to the left.

Just click in the Notes pane and begin typing or editing the text.

- Choose **View | Notes Page** to display a screen similar to the one below. You can then type or edit text for the currently selected slide.

Each notes page contains a miniature view of the slide and an area for working with text.

By default, PowerPoint displays a speaker notes page at about 38% of its full size. You may wish to increase this to nearer 100% when typing or editing.

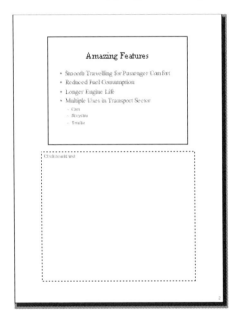

Exercise 3.7: Adding speaker notes

1 Open the green-on-yellow version of your first presentation. In Normal view, display its first slide, entitled 'Product Launch'.

2 Click in the Notes pane, and type the following text:

Introduce myself
Give special welcome to Mary

3 Click in the Slide pane, and use the Page Down key to display your fourth slide, entitled 'Choice of Colours'.

4 Change to Notes Page view, increase the Zoom magnification to 100%, and type the following text:

New colours will be announced shortly.

5 Return to Normal view. Save your presentation.

Handout pages

As you will learn in the final part of this chapter, you can, if you wish, simply print out your slides and distribute them to your audience.

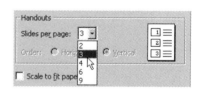

However, this is somewhat inelegant: the size of type that is appropriate for a slide is much too big for normal reading.

PowerPoint gives you the option of producing handouts in which two, three, four, six, or nine slides are shown to a page. A drop-down list on the Print dialog box allows you to specify the format you want to use.

Numbering your slides

When people in your audience ask questions, they may want to refer to a specific slide, so it is useful to identify each slide by number.

Exercise 3.8: Adding slide numbers

1 Display the yellow-on-blue version of your second presentation. In Normal view, choose **View | Header and Footer**.

2 In the Slide tab, select the Slide number checkbox.

Typically, you will not want PowerPoint to display the slide number on the title slide of your presentation. So select the Don't show on title slide checkbox. You can leave the other options unchecked.

3 Click **Apply to All**.

4 Switch to Slide Sorter view to confirm that PowerPoint has inserted numbers on all your slides. Save your presentation.

You can use the Notes and Handouts tab of the same dialog box to include page numbers on your speaker notes and audience handouts.

If you change the order of slides that contain slide numbers, PowerPoint automatically updates the slide numbers to reflect their new sequence.

If you want to display a particular slide in Slide Show view, just type the slide number and press Enter.

Formatting slide numbers

To change the font, font size or font colour of your slide numbers, display the slide master, and make your changes there. Exercise 3.9 provides an example.

Exercise 3.9: Formatting slide numbers

1   Display the yellow-on-blue version of your second presentation in Normal view, and choose **View Master | Slide Master** to display the slide master.

2   At the lower right of the slide master, click on the slide number symbol (#) to select it.

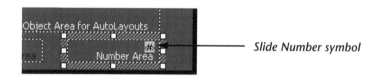

Slide Number symbol

3   Choose **Format | Font**, and change the text to Arial Black, Bold 14 points. Change the Colour to white. Click **OK**.

4   Change to Normal view to verify that your slide numbers have been reformatted. Save your presentation.

The story so far

You now have a total of *five* saved presentations, summarized in the following table.

Presentation topic	Presentation format	Suggested file name
Product Launch	Black text, white background	KBpres1.ppt
Product Launch	Medium green text, light yellow background	KBpres1_green_on_ yellow.ppt
Product Launch	Darker green text, preset decorative background of daybreak	KBpres1_daybreak.ppt
ECDL Overview	Black text, white background	KBpres2.ppt
ECDL Overview	Medium green, title text, medium yellow bullet text, dark blue background	KBpres2_yellow_on_blue.ppt

Printing your presentation

You can print out a PowerPoint presentation in a variety of ways, depending on your requirements and on the hardware at your disposal. Printing in PowerPoint is similar to printing in other applications:

Print button

- First, choose **File | Print**, or click the Print button on the Standard toolbar.

- Then, in the Print What drop-down box, you can choose to print slides, handouts, speaker notes, or the outline.

If you choose handouts, you
can choose the number of slides
per handout.

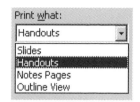

Whichever option you select, you can
then specify, in the Print range area of
the dialog box, whether you want to print all slides (or
handouts, notes, or the outline view), the current slide, or a
selected range of slides.

To print a contiguous range, type the number of the first
slide, a hyphen, and the number of the last slide. To print
non-contiguous slides, type the individual slide numbers
separated by commas.

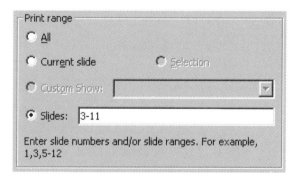

If you wish to produce overhead projection foils (OHPs), you
need to load your printer with blank foils before clicking **OK**
on the Print dialog box.

If you wish to produce 35mm slides, you need to have a
special desktop film recorder connected to your computer.

Landscape or portrait?

Most cinema, television, and computer screens are wider than they are tall: so will be most of your slide presentations. This format is known as *Landscape*; the alternative (taller) is known as *Portrait*.

If you ever want to produce a presentation in portrait format, choose **File | Page Setup**, and under Orientation, Slides, select Portrait, and click **OK**.

Exercise 3.10: Exercises in printing

1 Switch to the green-on-yellow version of your first 'Product Launch' presentation.

2 Print a set of handouts for the entire presentation with six slides on each page of the printout.

(As your presentation contains only five slides, this step prints your entire presentation on a single page.)

3 Print the first and fourth slide of your presentation.

4 Print the speaker notes for your first slide.

You can save and close all your presentations, and close PowerPoint. You have now completed Chapter 3 of the ECDL *Presentations* module.

Chapter summary: so now you know

Slide formatting refers to the appearance of slides and includes text formatting and background formatting behind the slide text.

Your text *formatting* options include making text bolder (heavier), putting it in italics, or placing a shadow behind it. You may also change the text font, size and colour. The two main *background formatting* options are dark text against a light background (good for lighted rooms) or light text against a dark background (good for darkened rooms). Backgrounds may consist of a solid, single-colour area or a decorative pattern.

You can change the appearance of an entire presentation by changing the text or background formatting on its *slide master*. A second method of reformatting a presentation is to apply one of PowerPoint's colour schemes – sets of preset text and background colours. You can customize *colour schemes*, combine colour schemes with slide master effects, and override colour scheme or slide master settings on any individual slide.

You can insert *slide numbers* on slides, to help you and your audience identify specific slides. PowerPoint automatically updates slides numbers as you add new slides and change the order of existing ones. You can format slide numbers in the slide master.

Speaker notes are pages that PowerPoint creates to accompany each slide. You can use them to record key points or additional details for the presenter.

PowerPoint gives you the option of producing printed *handouts* for your audience, in which two, three, four, six, or nine slides are shown to a page.

PowerPoint's *print options* enable you to print one, all or a range of slides, handouts, speaker notes or the outline. If you wish to produce overhead projection foils (OHPs), you need to load your printer with blank foils. To produce 35mm slides, you need to have a special desktop film recorder connected to your computer.

CHAPTER 4

Working with graphics and pictures

In this chapter

It's time to inject some visual flair into your presentations by discovering how to insert graphics and pictures on slides.

In this chapter, you will learn how to include pictures and other graphics in your slides.

New skills

At the end of this chapter, you should be able to:

- Draw simple graphics such as lines and boxes on a slide
- Draw AutoShapes on a slide
- Insert and use text boxes on a slide
- Insert clip art and other pictures on a slide
- Move, change the size and shape, rotate, group, and flip objects in a slide

- Apply line styles to lines and object borders, and fill colour and shadow effects on a slide
- Copy objects between slides

New words

At the end of this chapter you should be able to explain the following terms:

- AutoShapes
- Clip art

About graphics

The term 'graphics' includes plain and decorative lines, squares and rectangles, circles and ovals, and a wide variety of symbolic shapes.

You have two main options for including graphics in your slides:

- **Draw your own graphics**: You can use PowerPoint's drawing tools to create your own graphics.

- **Use built-in graphics**: PowerPoint includes AutoShapes – ready-made shapes such as flowchart elements, stars and banners, and callouts. You can select and include AutoShapes as supplied, or modify them to your taste or needs.

Drawing toolbar

Displayed along the bottom of your screen, the Drawing toolbar includes a number of tools for drawing simple objects, including lines, arrows, rectangles, and ellipses.

PowerPoint's Drawing toolbar

If the Drawing toolbar is not currently visible in Normal view, choose **View | Toolbars | Drawing** to display it.

Line and arrow tools

To draw a line, click the Line button, place the cursor where you want the line to begin, click and drag to where you want the line to end, and release the mouse button. 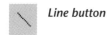 *Line button*

 Arrow button

To draw a line ending in an arrow, click on the Arrow button and draw it in the same way. *Arrow Style button*

To change the style of arrowhead, or the direction of the arrow, click the Arrow to select it, click the Arrow Style button, and select a different style.

Rectangle and square tool

To draw a rectangle, click the Rectangle button, place the cursor  *Rectangle and Square button*

where you want one corner of the rectangle, click and drag diagonally to where you want the opposite corner of the rectangle, and release the mouse button.

To draw a square, hold down the Shift key as you drag with the mouse.

Ellipse and circle tool

To draw an ellipse (oval), click the Ellipse button, place the cursor *Ellipse button*

where you want the shape to begin, click and drag until the shape is the size you want, and release the mouse button.

To draw a circle, hold down the Shift key as you drag with the mouse.

Line colour and style

In the case of lines, arrows, and *Line Color button*
closed shapes (such as rectangles
and circles), you can specify the colour and thickness of the
line or shape border. Click the arrow to the right of the Line
Color button and select a colour, either before you draw the
line or closed shape, or, with the line or shape selected, after
you have drawn it.

To delete a border around a closed shape, select **No Line** in
the line colour pop-up menu.

Change the thickness of a line *Line Style button*
or border by clicking the Line
Style button.

Make a line or border a dashed line
(in a choice of dash styles) by *Dash Style button*
clicking the Dash Style button.

Fill colour

Use the arrow to the right of the *Fill Color button*
Fill Color button to select the
colour with which the inside of
the selected closed shape (such as a
square or ellipse) should be filled.

Working with AutoShapes

AutoShapes are commonly-
used, ready-made shapes
that you can insert in your
presentations. AutoShape
categories include lines,
basic shapes, flowchart
elements, stars and banners,
and callouts.

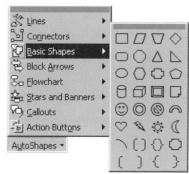

To select an AutoShape,
click the AutoShapes button on the Drawing toolbar and
choose from the options offered by the pop-up menu.

AutoShapes

Ready-made shapes, including lines, geometric shapes, and
flowchart elements that you can use in your presentations.

Working with objects

Lines, rectangles, circles, text boxes and AutoShapes are all
examples of what PowerPoint calls objects. So too are
placeholders, and inserted pictures, which you will meet later in
this chapter.

There are a number of common operations that you can
perform on objects, regardless of their type.

Moving objects

To move an object within the same slide, first select it by clicking anywhere on it. A cross appears at the tip of the cursor arrow. Then drag the object to its new position.

To move an object between slides, select it, and then cut and paste it.

Changing object size and shape

You can change the size and shape of an object by selecting it and clicking on any of its sizing handles. The cursor appears as a double arrow. Next, drag a sizing handle until the object is the new shape that you require.

Rotating and flipping objects

You can rotate a selected object through any angle to the left or right up through 360 degrees. You may rotate only objects created in PowerPoint, and not images or other items imported from another application.

Free Rotate button

To rotate a selected object, click the object to select it, and then click the Free Rotate button on the drawing toolbar. The border of the selected object disappears, and is replaced by four green dots, one at each corner.

Click on any of these and drag the object to its new orientation. (The cursor changes shape.) You can limit the object's rotation to 15° steps by holding down the Shift key as you drag with the mouse.

To flip (create a mirror image of) a selected object, click the Draw button on the drawing toolbar, choose **Rotate or Flip**, and then **Flip Horizontal** or **Flip Vertical**.

Shadow effects

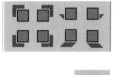

To place a shadow behind a selected object, click the Shadow button, and choose from the shadow styles available on the pop-up menu.

Shadow button

Grouping and ungrouping objects

You can group objects so that you can work with them as if they were a single object. For example, you can move, rotate or format grouped objects in a single operation.

To group objects, hold down the Shift key and click on each of the objects in turn. Next, click the Draw button on the Drawing toolbar and choose the **Group** command.

To ungroup a selected group of objects, click the Draw button on the Drawing toolbar and choose the Ungroup command.

Deleting objects

To delete any object or object group, click on it and press the Delete key. You can always reverse a deletion by clicking the Undo button on the Standard toolbar.

The following seven exercises provide examples of PowerPoint's graphics capabilities in action.

Exercise 4.1: Applying a border, fill and shadow to a placeholder in the slide master

1   If PowerPoint is not already open, open it now.

Open the 'Product Launch' presentation, with medium green text against a plain yellow background, which you created in Chapter 3. You named it as KBpres1_green_on_yellow.ppt or similar.

2   Choose **View | Master | Slide Master** to display your presentation's slide master.

3   Click anywhere in the top placeholder to select it, and then click anywhere on the placeholder border.

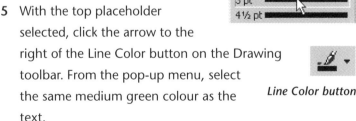

Notice how the border pattern changes when you click on it after selecting the placeholder.

4   Click the Line Style button on the drawing toolbar, and select a line width of 3 pt.

Line Style button

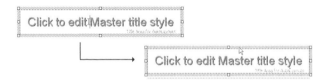

5   With the top placeholder selected, click the arrow to the right of the Line Color button on the Drawing toolbar. From the pop-up menu, select the same medium green colour as the text.

Line Color button

Switch to Slide Sorter view. Notice that the titles of all slides now have green borders around them.

6 Switch back to the slide master, click anywhere in the top placeholder, and click the arrow to the right of the Fill Color button on the Drawing toolbar.

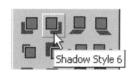

Fill Color button

From the pop-up menu displayed, choose **More Fill Colors**, and select a darker yellow than the slide background colour.

7 Switch to Slide Show view. Notice that the titles of all slides now have the darker yellow fill colour.

Finally, let's apply a shadow effect.

Shadow button

8 Switch back to the slide master, click anywhere in the top placeholder, and click the Shadow button on the Drawing toolbar.

From the pop-up menu displayed, select Shadow Style 6 (shadow beneath and to the right).

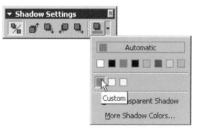

9 With the top placeholder selected, click the Shadow button on the Drawing toolbar. From the pop-up menu displayed, choose Shadow Settings, and click the arrow on the right of the **Shadow Settings** toolbar.

From the colours displayed, select the same medium green colour as the text. Close the Shadow Settings toolbar.

10   Switch to Slide Show view. Notice that the titles of all slides now have a shadowed green border and a dark yellow fill colour.

Product Launch

11   Save your presentation.

Well done. In a relatively few steps, you have changed the appearance of your entire presentation. Next, let's apply some graphic effects to just a single slide.

Exercise 4.2: Applying graphic effects to a placeholder on a single slide

1   In Normal view, display the title slide of the presentation that you worked on in Exercise 4.1.

Fill Color button

2   Click in the top placeholder to select it, click the arrow to the right of the Fill Color button on the Drawing toolbar, and select the same medium green colour as the text.

3   With the top placeholder selected, click the Shadow button on the Drawing toolbar. From the pop-up menu displayed, choose **No Shadow**. (This removes the shadow from the placeholder – not from the title text.)

4   Select the text in the upper placeholder by dragging across it with the mouse, and click the arrow to the right of the Font Color button on the Drawing toolbar.

Font Color button

From the pop-up menu displayed, select the same dark yellow that you applied to the title text placeholders in Exercise 4.1.

5   With the text still selected, click the Bold button on the Formatting toolbar. Your title should look as shown.

Product Launch

Save your presentation.

In the next exercise you will draw, copy, and group graphics, and then apply fills and borders to the grouped graphics.

Exercise 4.3: Drawing, copying, and grouping circles on a single slide

1   In Normal view, display the title slide of the presentation that you worked on in Exercises 4.1 and 4.2.

2   Click the Ellipse button on the Drawing toolbar, and hold down the Shift key.

Ellipse button

This ensures that the shape you are about to draw will be a circle rather than an oval.

3   Move the cursor over the slide and draw a small circle to the left of the words 'Round Wheels'.

If your circle is not positioned as shown, reposition it by dragging. (For small, precise movements, hold down the Ctrl key and use the arrow keys.)

4 With the circle selected, press Ctrl+c to copy it, and then Ctrl+v to paste it.

5 Drag your second circle over to the right of the words 'Round Wheels'.

6 With your second circle selected, hold down the Shift key, and click on your first circle. Both circles are now selected.

7 Click the Draw button on the left of the Drawing toolbar. From the pop-up menu displayed, choose **Group**.

You can now work with the two grouped graphics as if they were a single object.

8 Click the arrow to the right of the Fill Color button on the Drawing toolbar, and select the same medium green colour as the text.

Fill Color button

9 Click the arrow to the right of the Line Color button on the Drawing toolbar, and select the **No Line** option. This removes any border from the two grouped graphics.

Line Colour button

10 As a final step, click the Draw button on the left of the Drawing toolbar. From the pop-up menu displayed, choose **Ungroup**.

Well done. You have learnt how to draw and work with simple graphics on a slide. In the next exercise you will add a decorative line to all slides of your presentation.

Exercise 4.4: Inserting lines on all slides

1 Display the slide master of the presentation that you worked on in Exercises 4.1, 4.2 and 4.3.

2 Click the Line button on the Drawing toolbar. Move the cursor over the slide, and draw a line along the bottom of your slide master as shown.

Line button

3 With the line selected, click the Line Style button, and change the line thickness to 3pt.

Line Style button

4 Click the arrow to the right of the Line Color button on the Drawing toolbar. From the pop-up menu, select the same medium green colour as the text.

5 Switch to Slide Sorter view. Notice that all your slides now have a line along their lower edge.

Line Color button

In Normal view, your title slide should look as shown.

Save your presentation.

You have completed the exercises on your 'Product Launch' presentation. You can close this presentation if you wish.

In the remainder of this chapter, you will work with your 'ECDL: An Overview' presentation. You will begin by inserting one of PowerPoint's AutoShapes.

Exercise 4.5: Inserting an AutoShape on the slide master

1   Open the ECDL presentation, with yellow text against a dark blue background, which you created in Chapter 3. You named it as KBpres1_yellow_on_blue.ppt, or similar.

2   Choose **View | Master | Slide Master** to display the slide master for your presentation.

3 Click the AutoShapes button on the Drawing toolbar. From the pop-up menu displayed, choose **Stars and Banners,** and select the 5-Point Star.

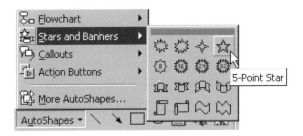

4 Draw the star in the lower right of the Object Area for AutoLayouts.

5 On the Standard toolbar, increase your Zoom magnification to 100%.

6 With the star selected, use the Fill Color button on the Drawing toolbar to change its fill colour to the same yellow as the text.

Fill Color button

7 With the star selected, use the Line Color button to change the star's border to yellow also.

8 With the star selected, press Ctrl+x to cut it, and then Ctrl+v to paste it. Press Ctrl+v twice again to paste the star a second and third time.

Line Color button

9   Reposition the three stars so that they are along a straight line in the bottom-right corner.

(For small movements, hold down the Ctrl key and press the arrow keys.)

10 Using their corner sizing handles, change the size of the left and middle stars, so that the first is smaller than the

second, and the second smaller than the third.

11 Switch to Slide Sorter view. Notice that each slide now has three stars in its lower right corner.

In exactly the same way, you can import any graphic or other object directly into your slide master, or copy (or cut) and paste an object from another presentation or from another application program. You can then reposition and resize the object as above.

Text boxes

Up to now, you have entered text on slides by selecting a placeholder and then typing text into it. You can also enter text by drawing a text box and then typing text into that.

You can change the format and alignment of text in a text box in the same way as you would text in a placeholder.

Note, however, that PowerPoint does not display text entered in a text box in the Outline pane.

Exercise 4.6: Inserting a text box

1 In Normal view, display the title (first) slide of the presentation that you worked on in Exercise 4.5. Change the Zoom setting so that you can see the whole slide on your screen.

2 Click the Text Box button on the Drawing toolbar, and draw a text box in the lower left corner of the slide.

Text Box button

3 Select the text box and type the following:

Best Results

4 Select the text, and change it to Arial, Bold, 24 points.

If the text does not fit on a single line in your text box, click on a corner of the box and drag to make the box wider.

5 With the text selected, change its colour to the same medium green as the slide titles.

Click anywhere else on the slide to deselect the text box.

Exercise 4.7: Rotating a text box

1 Click the text box that you created in Exercise 4.6 to select it.

2 Click the Free Rotate button on the Drawing toolbar. Notice how PowerPoint replaces the border of the text box by four green dots, one at each corner.

3 Click on the top-left green dot, and rotate the text box by about 45 degrees. Press the Esc key to switch off the rotation feature.

Your rotated text should look as shown.

Save your presentation.

Well done. You have now finished your exercises in PowerPoint graphics. It's time to learn about importing pictures.

Importing pictures

You can also illustrate your slides by inserting pictures – drawings created in other software applications, scanned photographs, or clip art.

PowerPoint includes a gallery of clip art pictures that you can use in different presentations. They are grouped in categories, ranging from academic to food and transportation.

Clip Art

Standard or 'stock' images that can be used and reused in presentations and other documents.

You can include a picture in a slide in any of the following ways:

• Create a new slide, and select either of the following two AutoLayouts:

 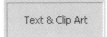   

PowerPoint displays the Clip Art icon on
your slide. Double-click the Clip Art icon,
click on a picture category to view the
individual pictures available, right-click
on a picture, and choose **Insert** from the
pop-up menu.

Clip Art icon

–or–

• Display an existing slide, and do either of the following:

  – Choose **Insert | Picture | Clip Art**, and select a
  picture from the range displayed.

    –or–

  – Choose **Format | Slide Layout**, select either of the
  two AutoLayouts shown above, and click **Apply**.
  Double-click the Clip Art icon, and select the picture
  that you require.

You will practise working with pictures in the next two exercises.

Exercise 4.8: Inserting a clip art picture

1 In Normal view, display the presentation that
you worked on in Exercise 4.7, and display the third
slide, entitled 'Benefits for Colleges'.

2 Choose **Format | Slide Layout**, and select the
AutoLayout named Clip Art & Text, and click **Apply**.

Your slide should now look as shown opposite. Notice
how PowerPoint automatically reduces the font size of
the bullet points.

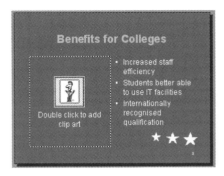

3   Double-click on the Clip Art icon to open the Microsoft Clip Art Gallery, and click on the Academic category.

4   From the Academic category, right-click on the Graduation picture, and choose Insert from the pop-up menu displayed.

PowerPoint inserts the picture in your slide.

5   Click on the lower-right handle of the inserted picture and reduce it in size by about 20%.

Your slide should look like that shown.

6   In Normal view, display your fifth slide, entitled 'Benefits for Employers'. Choose **Insert | Picture | Clipart** and click the Business category.

7   Right-click on the Working Towards Goals picture, and choose Insert from the pop-up menu. Click the Close button at the top right of the Insert Clip Art window: it does not close

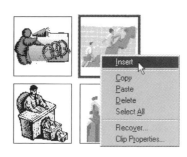

automatically when you are using the **Insert | Picture | Clip Art** command.

PowerPoint has inserted the picture in your slide.

8   Reduce your inserted picture in size by about 20%, and move it to the centre of the lower part of your slide.

Your slide should look as shown.

9   With your fifth slide still displayed in Normal view, click the New Slide button on the Standard toolbar.

10   Select the AutoLayout named Text & Clip Art, and click **OK**.

11 In the title placeholder of your new, sixth slide, type the following:

Benefits for Society

In the text placeholder, type the following:

Participation for all in the Information Society

12 Double-click on the Clip Art icon to open the Microsoft Clip Art Gallery, and click on the Home & Family category.

13 Right-click on the Seniors picture, and choose Insert from the pop-up menu.

PowerPoint inserts the picture in your slide.

14 Click on the lower-right handle of the inserted picture and reduce it in size by about 20%.

Drag the picture up until it is level with the bullet point text in the left placeholder.

Your slide should look like that shown.

15   Choose **View | Slide Show,** or click the Slide Show
     button. Move forward and back through your
     presentation to see how it would look to the audience.

You can move, resize, or delete an imported image as you
would any other object, and, as the next exercise shows, you
can place borders and shadows around them.

Exercise 4.9: Placing borders and shadows around pictures

1   In Normal view, display the presentation that you
    worked on in Exercise 4.8, and display your third
    slide, entitled 'Benefits for Colleges'.

Line Style button

2   Click the inserted picture to select it.

3   Click the Line Style button
    on the Drawing toolbar.
    From the menu displayed,
    select a line width of 1 point.

    PowerPoint places a 1 point
    solid border around your
    inserted picture.

4   With the picture selected,
    click the Line Color button,
    and change its colour to the same green as the
    slide title text.

Line Color button

5   Display your sixth slide, entitled
    'Benefits for Society'. Click the inserted picture to select it.

6 Click the Shadow button on the Drawing toolbar. From the pop-up menu displayed, select the Shadow Style 2 option.

PowerPoint places a shadow around your inserted picture.

Fill Color button

7 With the inserted picture selected, click again on the Shadow button on the Drawing toolbar, and select the **Shadow Settings** option to view the Shadow Settings toolbar.

8 Click the arrow at the right of the Shadow Settings toolbar, choose **More Shadow Colors**, and select a light blue from the colours available.

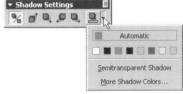

9 PowerPoint places a light blue shadow around your imported picture. Close the shadow settings toolbar and save your presentation.

Well done! You have completed the picture exercises in PowerPoint.

Non Clip Art pictures

To insert an image of your own – your company logo, for example – on a slide, choose **Insert | Picture | From File**, select the required image file, and choose **Insert**.

PowerPoint accepts images in most common image file formats.

The Picture toolbar

To change the colours, brightness, or contrast of the picture, you can use the picture toolbar. Either choose **View | Toolbars | Picture**, or right-click on the picture and choose the **Show Picture Toolbar** option.

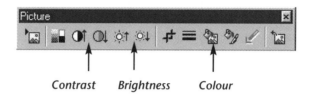

    Contrast   Brightness   Colour

Any changes you make are shown on-screen. Click on the Close box at the top-right of the Picture toolbar when you are finished.

Experiment on your three inserted pictures using the Picture toolbar. You can reverse any changes you make with the Undo button.

You may now save and close all open presentations, and close PowerPoint. You have completed Chapter 4 of the ECDL *Presentations* module.

Chapter summary: so now you know

The *graphics* that you can draw on PowerPoint slides include simple shapes such as lines, arrows, rectangles, circles, and ellipses. *AutoShapes* are commonly used, ready-made shapes that you can insert in your presentations. AutoShape categories include lines, basic shapes, flowchart elements, stars and banners, and callouts.

You can change the shape, size, position and colour of simple graphics and AutoShapes. You can rotate them, flip them, and add shadows behind them. You can also group them so that you can work with them as if they were single objects.

A *text box* is a text placeholder that you insert directly on a slide. You can change the format and alignment of text in a text box in the same way as you would text in a placeholder that is part of an AutoLayout.

You can illustrate your slides by inserting *pictures* – drawings created in other software applications or scanned photographs. PowerPoint includes a gallery of *clip art* pictures that you can use in different presentations.

You can move, resize or delete an imported picture as you would any other object, and place borders and shadows around them.

CHAPTER 5

Working with tables and charts

In this chapter

You are not limited to creating slides with bullet points in PowerPoint. In this chapter you will learn about three other types of slides that are suited for presenting particular types of information: slides with *tables,* slides with *organization charts*, and slides with *quantitative charts*.

Tables consist of rectangular cells of text or numbers, arranged in rows and columns. Organization charts are suitable for showing the roles of people in an organization (represented by boxes) and their relationships (represented by lines). Quantitative (number-based) charts include the bar, column and pie chart types.

New skills

At the end of this chapter you should be able to:
- Create, enter text on, and format a table on a slide
- Create, enter text on, and format an organization chart on a slide
- Modify the structure of an organization chart
- Create bar, column and pie charts for presenting quantitative information
- Reformat the appearance of a chart or selected chart elements
- Change a chart's type

New words

At the end of this chapter you should be able to explain the following terms:
- Organization chart

Working with tables

You can create a table in PowerPoint in the following ways:

- On an existing slide, click the Insert Table button on the Standard toolbar.

  Insert Table button

  Next, drag to select the number of rows and columns you want.

  –or–

- On an existing slide, choose the **Insert | Table** command, select the number of rows and columns required, and click **OK**.

  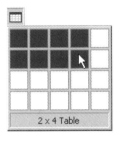

  –or–

- Create a new slide and select the AutoLayout named Table. PowerPoint displays the Table icon on your slide. Double-click it, select the number of rows and columns you require, and click **OK**.

  Table icon

As with text in a text box, PowerPoint does not display text in a table in the Outline pane of Normal view.

Exercise 5.1: Inserting a table

1 If PowerPoint is not already open, open it now. Open the ECDL presentation, with yellow text against a dark blue background, which you worked with in Chapter 4. You named it as KBpres2_yellow_on_blue.ppt or similar.

New Slide
button

2 Display your sixth slide, entitled 'Benefits for Society', click the New Slide button on the Standard toolbar, select the AutoLayout named Table, and click **OK**.

Double-click the table icon, select 2 columns and 4 rows, and click **OK**.

Type text in your slide until it looks as shown below.

3 Select the top row of your table by dragging across the two top table cells with the mouse.

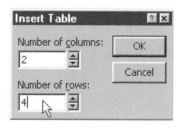

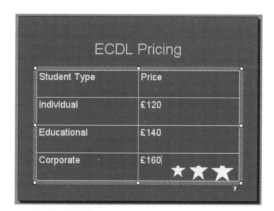

4   With the top row selected, click the Bold button and
    then the Centre-align button on the Formatting toolbar.

5   With the top row still selected, use the Fill Color
    button on the Drawing toolbar, and change its
    colour to the same medium green as
    the slide title text.

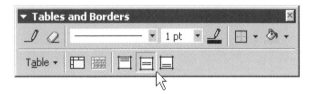

Fill Color button

6   With the top row still selected, choose **View | Toolbars |
    Tables and Borders**.

On the toolbar, select the centre vertically option. Close
the Tables and Borders toolbar.

7   Select the three cells containing prices, and click the
    Centre-align button on the Formatting toolbar.

8   With the table placeholder selected, click the centre
    sizing handle on the lower placeholder border. Your
    cursor changes to a double-header arrow.

9   Drag the sizing handle upwards until the table
    placeholder no longer overlaps the three stars.

    Click anywhere else on the slide to deselect the
    table placeholder.

    Your slide should look as shown overleaf.

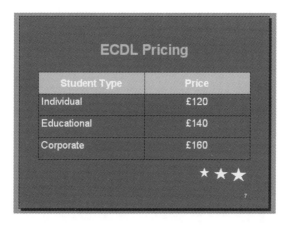

10   Save your presentation, which now has seven slides.

Organization charts

Organization charts are used to illustrate people's positions within an organization or the structure of components within a physical system or process. Such charts have two main components:

- **Boxes**: These represent people in the organization or components within the system or process.

- **Lines**: These represent relationships between people or units of the organization or system.

You could create organization charts using the drawing tools, but such charts are used so frequently that PowerPoint provides a tool especially for producing them.

Organization chart

> *A diagram used to illustrate the people or units in an organization or system (represented by boxes) and their relationships (represented by lines).*

To include an organization chart in a slide:

- Choose **Insert | New Slide** or click the New Slide button on the Standard toolbar.

- Select the AutoLayout named Organization Chart and click **OK**.

- PowerPoint displays the Organization Chart icon on your slide. Double-click it.

Organization Chart icon

PowerPoint opens a new window that displays an organization chart template and offers new menus of commands. For example:

- The **Styles** menu allows you to choose different chart types

- The **Text, Boxes** and **Lines** menus each allow you format the respective chart elements.

You can alter the template as you wish. Although the boxes have text labels in them, such as 'Type name here', you can enter any type of information in any box – the labels are for your guidance only.

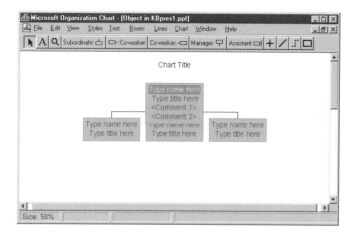

Exercise 5.2: Inserting an organization chart

1 In Normal view, display the slide, entitled 'ECDL Pricing', that you created in Exercise 5.1.

2 Click the New Slide button on the standard toolbar, select the Organization Chart AutoLayout, and click **OK**.

New Slide button

3 Click in the title placeholder, and type: ABC Sales Team.

4 Double-click the Organisation Chart icon to open the Organization Chart window.

5 Type text in the template as shown.

6   When you have finished working in the Organisation
    Chart window, return to your slide by choosing **File |
    Exit and Return to,** and then clicking **Yes** on the dialog
    box displayed.

Within PowerPoint, you can move, resize, place borders or
shadows around, or delete a chart as you would any other
object. To make any other changes to the chart, however, you
have to double-click on the chart and make your changes in
the Organization Chart window.

Exercise 5.3: Reformatting an organization chart

1   Display your organization chart slide in Normal view,
    and select the chart by clicking anywhere on it.

2   As you learnt in Chapter 4, you can make text and
    graphics on your slides appear to stand out from the
    background by adding a shadow to them.

    Click the Shadow button on the Drawing toolbar. From
    the menu displayed, select Shadow Style 5.

3   With the chart still selected, click the Shadow button
    again. From the pop-up menu displayed, choose
    Shadow Settings. On the Shadow Settings toolbar, click
    the arrow to the right of the Shadow Color button, and
    select light blue as the shadow colour.

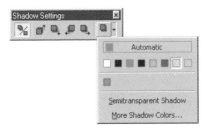

Close the shadow settings button bar.

Be careful when choosing a colour for the shadow that you do not interfere with the legibility of your text. Save your presentation.

Exercise 5.4: Modifying the structure of an organization chart

1 In Normal view, display the organization chart slide that you created in Exercise 5.2. Double-click on the organization chart.

2 The chart is opened in the Organization Chart window. The toolbar provides buttons for adding boxes (Subordinates, Co-workers, Managers, Assistants) and lines.

Click the second Co-worker button.

3 Next, click the box containing Graham Horton. A new box is created, at the same level in the hierarchy, and the other chart elements are rearranged.

4 Click the new box, and enter text as shown below.

5   Close the Organization Chart window, and confirm that you want to update the chart in the presentation.

Charts

PowerPoint provides a variety of bar, column, pie and other chart types that are useful for presenting quantitative (number-based) information

To include a chart in a slide:

*   Choose **Insert | New Slide** or click the New Slide button on the Standard toolbar.

*   Select any of the three chart AutoLayouts that contains chart placeholders, and click **OK**.

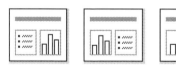

*   Double-click the Chart icon.

When you insert a chart, PowerPoint displays the following:

Chart icon

- **Datasheet**: A small spreadsheet that you can adapt by typing in your own text and numbers, over-writing those already present. You can add or delete rows or columns as you require.

  You can move the datasheet to a different part of your screen by clicking and dragging its title bar.

- **Chart**: This changes as you change the contents of the datasheet.

  You can change the colour or format of any element in the chart by double-clicking on it: you are presented with options that are relevant to that element.

- **Chart menus**: Excel-like menus of charting commands appear at the top of the PowerPoint window.

  You can close the datasheet window by clicking anywhere else on the PowerPoint screen.

Datasheet

Chart

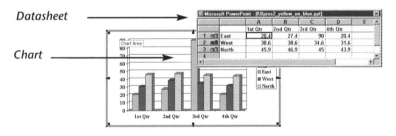

Chart type options

Perhaps your most important decision with a chart is the selection of the appropriate chart type. The most commonly used types are column, line, and pie.

- **Column charts**: These are typically used to show figures that are measured at a particular time.

- **Line charts**: These are typically used to illustrate trends over time.

- **Pie charts**: These are typically used to illustrate the breakdown of figures in a total. A pie chart is always based on a *single* column of numbers.

To change the chart type:

- If the Datasheet window is not already open, double-click the chart to open it.

- Right-click on the chart and, from the pop-up menu displayed, choose **Chart Type**.

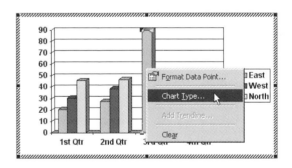

- Select the chart type and sub-type from the list in the Standard Types tab of the dialog box.

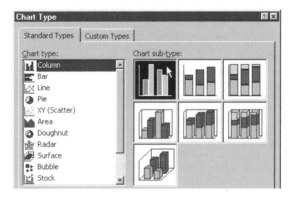

- Click **OK**.

PowerPoint gives you a wide variety of presentation options for charts. Some of them, however, are more decorative than informative: be careful that your message isn't obscured.

Exercise 5.5: Inserting a chart

1   In Normal view, display the organization chart slide that you worked on in Exercise 5.4.

2   Click the New Slide button on the Standard toolbar, select the AutoLayout named Chart, and click **OK**.

3   Click in the title text placeholder and type the following text:

Sales Projections

4   Double-click the Chart icon to open the Datasheet window.

5 Edit the text in the datasheet as shown. You can resize the Datasheet window at any stage by clicking on its lower-right corner and dragging.

		A	B	C	D	
		1st Qtr	2nd Qtr	3rd Qtr	4th Qtr	
1	Europe	1000	1200	1300	1400	
2	North America	1200	1500	1400	1300	
3	Asia/Pacific	750	750	250	250	
4	Rest of World	750	750	750	750	
5						

KBpres2.ppt - Datasheet

Notice how the chart changes as you edit and type text.

You will need to make the first column wider by clicking its boundary in the column header, and then dragging the boundary to the right.

6 When you have finished working in the Datasheet window, close it. You are returned to your slide.

7 Save your presentation.

Click anywhere else on your slide to deselect the chart placeholder.

Your slide should look as shown.

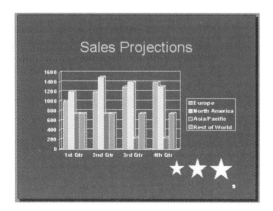

Sometimes, you may wish to change the colour of an element of a chart (such as a column in a column chart, a bar in a bar chart, or a 'slice' in a pie chart). Perhaps the colour you want to change does not contrast sufficiently with your slide background colour – or maybe you just don't like the colour.

The next exercise shows you how to change the colour of a chart column, and the colours of the chart axes and chart legend.

Exercise 5.6: Reformatting a chart

1 In Normal view, display the chart slide that you created in Exercise 5.5.

Double-click on the chart, and then right-click on any column of the chart. From the pop-up menu displayed, choose **Format Data Series**.

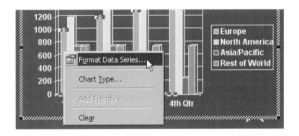

2 On the Patterns tab of the dialog box displayed, select white as the color, and click **OK**.

PowerPoint changes the colour of the column to white.

Next, let's change the colour of the axes, axes text, and legend text.

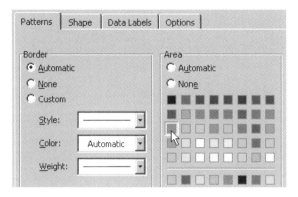

3   With the chart selected, right-click on the vertical axis and choose **Format Axis** from the pop-up menu.

4   On the Font tab of the dialog box displayed, click the arrow to the right of the Color box, select white, and click **OK**.

5   With the chart selected, repeat Steps 3 and 4 for the chart's horizontal axis.

6   With the chart selected, right-click on the chart legend, choose **Format Legend**, and, on the Font tab, change the legend text colour to white.

Within PowerPoint, you can move, resize or delete a chart as you would any other object. To make changes to the data in the chart, however, you have to double-click on the chart and make your changes in the Datasheet window.

   In the next exercise you will change the chart type from a column chart (the PowerPoint default) to a bar chart.

Exercise 5.7: Changing chart type

1   In Normal view, display the chart slide that you worked on in Exercise 5.6.

Double-click the chart to select it.

2   Right-click anywhere in the area surrounding the chart within the chart placeholder. From the pop-up menu displayed, choose Chart Type.

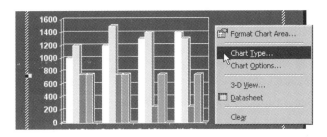

3   In the Chart Type dialog box, select Bar as the chart type, click the first chart sub-type, and click **OK**.

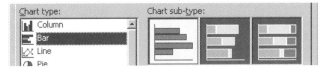

PowerPoint changes the chart type from column to bar.

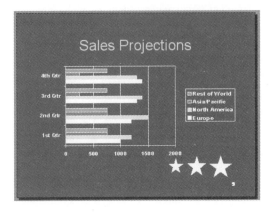

Exercise 5.8: Inserting a pie chart

1 In Normal view, display the chart slide that you worked on in Exercise 5.7.

2 Click the New Slide button on the standard toolbar, select the AutoLayout named Chart, and click **OK**.

3 Click in the title text placeholder and type the following text:

Annual Sales Growth

4 Double-click the Chart icon to open the Datasheet window.

# KBpres2_yellow_on_blue.ppt - Datasheet		A	B	C	D	E
		1998	1999	2000	2001	
1 ▣ 3-D Colum		12	15	19	21	
2 ▣ 3-D Colum						
3 ▣ 3-D Colum						
4						

5 Edit the text as shown in the datasheet.

To remove sample numbers and text that PowerPoint has placed in cells, click in each cell and press the Delete key. When finished, close the datasheet and return to your slide.

6 Right-click on any column of your chart, choose **Chart Type** from the pop-up menu, select Pie as Chart type, select the first chart sub-type, and click **OK**.

7 With the chart selected, right-click in the Plot Area – the area outside the pie shape but inside the chart area.

8   From the pop-up menu displayed, choose **Format Plot Area.**

9   On the dialog box displayed, select None for Border, and click **OK.**

10 With the chart selected, right-click on the chart legend, choose **Format Legend,** and, on the Font tab, change the legend text colour to white.

11 Right-click anywhere on the pie chart and choose **Format Data Series.** On the Data Labels tab, select Show value and click **OK.**

12 Click anywhere else on the slide to deselect the chart. Your slide should now look as shown.

Save your presentation.

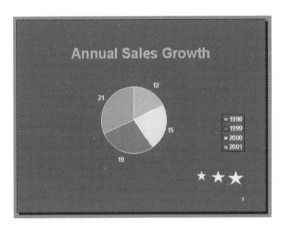

13 Switch to Slide Show view, and inspect your ten-slide presentation as it will be seen by your audience. Impressive, eh?

You may now save and close all open presentations, and close PowerPoint. You have completed Chapter 5 of the ECDL *Presentations* module.

Chapter summary: so now you know

You can create a *table* on a slide with a selected number of rows and columns, enter numbers and text headings, and apply formatting to it.

Organization charts are used to illustrate people's positions within an organization or the structure of components within a physical system or process. Such charts consist of boxes (for representing people or components) and lines (for representing their relationships). PowerPoint's organization chart tool provides a customizable chart template, with boxes arranged in a hierarchical structure.

You can present quantitative (number-based) information in a variety of *chart types*, such as bar, column, and pie charts. PowerPoint's chart-creating tool includes a *datasheet* (a small spreadsheet into which you can type your own text and numbers) and chart menus with relevant spreadsheet-like commands.

Your chart changes as you modify the contents of the datasheet. You can change the colour or format of any element in the chart (such as a column in a column chart, the chart axes or the chart legend) by double-clicking on it, and choosing an option from the menu displayed.

You can move, resize, and place borders or shadows around an organization chart or quantitative data chart as you would any other slide object.

CHAPTER 6

Wowing your audience

In this chapter

Your slides may contain convincing content, attractive colours and backgrounds, and impressive charts, yet may still lack something. That 'something' – call it *movement* – is what you learn about in this section.

You will discover how you can make your slides advance automatically after a specified time interval, insert visual transition effects between slides, and animate slide elements, both text and graphics, so that they appear progressively rather than all at once.

Animations, as you will learn, are more than a visual effect. By enabling the presenter to highlight each point on a slide in turn, they help to focus the audience's attention.

New skills

At the end of this section, you should be able to:

- Apply manual, timed automatic and 'whichever comes first' slide advance methods
- Specify the nature and timing of transition effects
- Apply preset animations
- Customize animation effects so as to modify the order, direction, sound effect and dim effect of animations
- Include graphics and pictures in animations
- Animate elements within a chart
- Check the spellings in your presentation

New words

At the end of this section you should be able to explain the following terms:

- Advance method
- Slide transition
- Animated slide

Automatic or manual advance?

When presenting your slides to your audience, you don't need to press Page Down or click with the mouse each time you want to move from the current slide.

Here's another option: get PowerPoint to run the show for you, so that your presentation proceeds automatically. You are then free to stand back from your computer and interact more directly your audience.

Automatic advance, available with the **Slide Show | Slide Transition** command, is often used in presentations that are left running in public areas, such as trade shows, where they are not accompanied by a speaker.

Whichever comes first

You can combine the manual and automatic advance methods so that the presenter can directly override the automatic, timed advance at any stage.

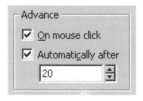

To do so, apply a timed advance, but also select the On mouse click checkbox.

(When On mouse click is selected, pressing Page Down or Enter will also display the next slide.)

Exercise 6.1: Applying an advance method to a presentation

1   If PowerPoint is not already open, open it now.

2   Open the ECDL presentation with yellow text against a dark blue background, which you worked with in Chapter 5. You named it as KBpres2_yellow_on_blue.ppt, or similar.

3   With any slide open in Normal view, choose **Slide Show | Slide Transition**.

4   In the dialog box displayed, in the Advance area, click Automatically after, and then type the number of seconds (for example, 15) that you want each slide to appear on-screen.

5   Ensure that the On mouse click checkbox is selected. In the Sound drop-down list, select Applause.

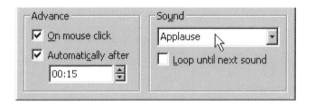

6   Click **Apply to All** to apply the automatic slide advance to your entire presentation. Save your presentation.

7   Choose **View | Slide Show** and see how your selected advance methods affect the running of your presentation.

Advance method

The way that PowerPoint displays the slides of a presentation: manually, automatically, or automatically with manual override. Automatic advance is often used for unaccompanied presentations.

Slide transitions

A transition is a graphic effect that controls how one slide replaces another – for example, the new slide could appear to drop down from the top of the screen, or the old slide could be made to dissolve, revealing the new slide.

PowerPoint lets you select two aspects of a transition:

Some transition options

- **Effect type**: The nature of the special effect with which PowerPoint introduces the slide.

- **Effect timing**: The speed with which PowerPoint runs the visual effect when introducing the slide.

Optionally, for added impact, you can also link a sound to the transition between slides. Exercise 6.2 provides an example.

Transition

A visual effect, such as a drop-down, box-out, dissolve, or fade, that controls how one slide in a presentation is replaced by another.

Exercise 6.2: Applying a transition to a presentation

1 In Normal view, display any slide of the presentation that you worked on in Exercise 6.1. Choose **Slide Show | Slide Transition**.

2 First explore the transition options on offer:

- **Effect**: Each time you click an option from the drop-down list, PowerPoint runs the effect in the sample picture. You can rerun the preview by clicking the picture.

- **Timing**: The options – Slow, Medium or Fast – set the speed at which the transition effect runs. Click an option and PowerPoint runs the effect with that timing in the sample picture.

   For this exercise, select the effect named Dissolve, with Fast Timing.

3 Click **Apply to All**.

   Notice that PowerPoint gives you the option of applying a different transition to each slide (by clicking **Apply**), but be careful: this option may have the effect of distracting or unsettling your audience.

4 See how the transitions affect the presentation by choosing **View | Slide Show** and moving through the presentation. Save your presentation, and leave it open. You will use it again in Exercise 6.5.

Slide advance methods and transition effects

You specify the slide advance method and the slide transition effects in the Slide Transitions dialog box. The two effects are independent, however:

- You can automate the running of your slide show without applying a transition.

- You can apply a transition without automating your slide show.

Also, the timings have nothing to do with one another:

- Effect timing (slow, medium, fast) controls the speed of the transition from the previous slide.

- Automated advance time specifies how long the slide is displayed before being replaced.

Animated slides

Animated slides are slides on which the information – typically, bullet points – is revealed gradually rather than all at once. When you first show the slide, the audience sees only the first bullet. You then reveal the remaining bullets, one-by-one, as you talk to your audience.

With an animated slide, you can highlight each point in turn to focus your audience's attention. When you are talking about your second point, for example, you can leave the first one on the screen, but dim it, so that it still serves as a context and reminder, but doesn't distract.

Animated slide

A slide in which different elements are revealed at different times.

You can create animated slides using either of the following two methods:

- **Preset animations**: A series of 13 ready-to-go animations, some with associated sound effects, which you can quickly apply to your slides.

- **Custom animations**: These offer a wide range of dynamic effects and options.

Preset animation options

Animated slides enable you to keep your audience engaged with what you are saying, rather than having them read ahead while you are still talking about the first point.

Animations and the slide master

To apply an animation to an entire presentation, first display your slide master, and then apply the preset or custom animation. Let's begin by applying a preset animation to a slide master.

Exercise 6.3: Applying a preset animation to a presentation

1   Open the Product Launch presentation, with dark green text against a daybreak effect background, which you worked with in Chapter 3. You named it as KBpres1_daybreak.ppt or similar.

2   Choose **View Master | Slide Master** to display your presentation's slide master.

3   Click anywhere in the lower placeholder, where the bulleted text is.

4   Choose **Slide Show | Preset Animation** and select the option called **Drive-In**.

| O̲ff |
| ✓ D̲rive-In |
| F̲lying |
| C̲amera |

5   Choose **View | Slide Show** and move through your slides to view the animation effect.

Remember: you need to click the mouse (or press Page Down or Enter) for each bullet point to appear.

6   Save your presentation.

In the next exercise, you will change some settings applied by the preset animation.

Exercise 6.4: Customizing a preset animation

1   Display the Product Launch presentation that you worked on in Exercise 6.3. Choose **View Master | Slide Master** and click anywhere in the lower placeholder.

2   Choose **Slide Show | Custom Animation**. The dialog box displayed shows the settings of the preset animation, and gives you the ability to change them.

3   On the Effects tab, replace the From Right setting with From Left, and the Screeching Brakes sound effect with [No Sound].

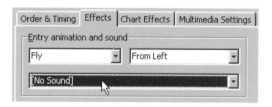

Next, in the After animation box, select medium green.

4   Click on the Order & Timing tab, and select the On mouse click option. Click **OK**. Save your presentation.

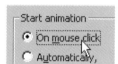

5   Choose **View | Slide Show** and move through your slides to view the animation effect. You can close this presentation when finished.

Customizing preset animations

As you can see when you run your presentation, you have customized the animation effects in the following ways:

- **Direction**: The bullet points now move onto the slides from the left edge rather than from the right.

- **Sound**: You have removed the sound effect associated with the animation.

- **Dim effect**: As soon as a new bullet point appears, PowerPoint changes the previous one to a less prominent colour. This 'dimming' effect helps your audience to focus on the flow of your presentation.

Many PowerPoint users find it best to follow the approach of Exercises 6.3 and 6.4. They first apply a present animation that is close to what they want, and then they use the custom animation command to make adjustments where necessary.

Music and other noises

In the same way that you can insert pictures other than those in Microsoft's clip art gallery on slides, you are not limited to using only those sound effects that are supplied with PowerPoint.

On the Sounds drop-down list on the Effects tab of the **Slide Show | Custom Animation** dialog box, you can see the Other Sound… option. To associate a sound with an animation, click this option and select any file that has the extension .wav.

In the remaining exercises in this section, you will apply animation effects to your yellow-on-blue ECDL presentation.

Exercise 6.5: Applying and Customising Animation Effects

1 Display the yellow-on-blue ECDL presentation that you last worked on in Exercise 6.2.

2 Choose **View Master | Slide Master** and click in the top (Title Area for AutoLayouts) placeholder.

3 Choose **Slide Show | Preset Animation** and select the option named Flying.

4 Click anywhere in the lower (Object Area for AutoLayouts) placeholder, choose **Slide Show | Preset Animation** and again select the option named Flying.

5 With the lower placeholder still selected, choose **Slide Show | Custom Animation**. On the Effects tab, change the After animation setting to a light blue colour, and click **OK** to close the Custom Animation dialog box.

6 Save your presentation. Choose **View | Slide Show** and page through your presentation.

Notice that the animations have no impact on your slide transitions – the two visual effects, and any associated sounds, are independent.

Including tables, pictures and charts in animations

The presentation that you worked on in Exercise 6.5 has one table, three inserted pictures, one organization chart, and two data charts.

As you ran the presentation, did you notice that the following were *not* animated by PowerPoint:

• The picture on slide 5, 'Benefits for Employers'

• The table on slide 7, 'ECDL Pricing'?

That is, the table and picture each appeared as soon the relevant slide was displayed. Yet all the other pictures and the charts appeared only after you clicked the mouse or pressed Enter. What is going on?

The answer is that PowerPoint, by default, animates only those pictures and charts that are inserted within the appropriate slide layout (such as Text & Clip Art, Organization Chart or Chart). PowerPoint animates the picture or chart by default.

The picture on slide 5, however, was included on its slide with the **Insert | Picture | Clip Art** command.

Also by default, PowerPoint does not animate tables. As you will discover in Exercise 6.6, PowerPoint gives you complete control over table, picture and chart animations.

Exercise 6.6: Including picture and charts in animations

1 Display the yellow-on-blue presentation that you last worked on In Exercise 6.5.

2 In Normal view, display the 'Benefits for Colleges' slide. Click anywhere on the slide and choose **Slide Show | Custom Animation**.

On the Order & Timing tab, notice that the picture, which PowerPoint calls Object 3, is included in the animation order.

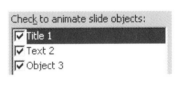

3 Repeat Step 2 for the following slides: 'Benefits for Society', 'ABC Sales Team, 'Sales Projections', and 'Annual Sales Growth'. In each case, you can see that the picture or chart is included in the animation order.

4 Display the 'Benefits for Employers' slide, choose **Slide Show | Custom Animation**, and click the Order & Timing tab. Notice that the picture is not animated.

Before   *After*

Click Picture frame 3 to select it, and click **OK** to close the dialog box.

5   Display the 'ECDL Pricing' slide and choose **Slide Show | Custom Animation**. On the Order & Timing tab, include the table in the animation order, and click **OK**.

6   Save your presentation. Choose **View | Slide Show** and page through your presentation to see the effect on the 'Benefits for Employers' and 'ECDL Pricing' slides. Save your presentation.

Animating charts

As you have seen, you can include a chart in a slide animation, or exclude it if you prefer. But PowerPoint offers yet another animation feature regarding charts – it allows you to animate the elements **within** a chart, so that chart element are displayed progressively rather than all at once.

Exercise 6.7: Animating the Elements of a Chart

1   Display the yellow-on-blue presentation that you worked on in Exercise 6.6. In Normal view, display the 'Sales Projections' slide.

2   Click once on the chart to select it, choose **Slide Show | Custom Animation**, and click the Chart Effects tab.

3   Experiment with the various settings, clicking the **Preview** button to see their effect on your chart.

Now select the settings as shown, and click **OK** to close the dialog box.

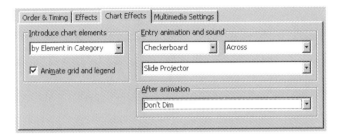

4   Save your presentation. Choose **View | Slide Show** and page through your presentation to see the effect on the 'Sales Projections' slide.

Check your spelling!

Spelling mistakes really spoil a presentation: they make you look either careless or ignorant – and your effort to impress the audience may be wasted. While it is dangerous to rely totally on a spellchecker, it is also foolish not to use one at all.

In PowerPoint, you can check your spelling in two ways:

- As you type and edit text on slides (the automatic option). Wavy underlines indicate words with possible spelling errors. To correct the spelling, right-click a wavy line, and then choose the option you want from the pop-up menu displayed.

- Whenever you choose **Tools | Spelling**, press **F7** or click the Spelling button on the toolbar (the on-request option).

Spelling button

To turn automatic spellchecking on or off, choose **Tools |
Options** and select or deselect the Check spelling as you type
checkbox on the Spelling and Style tab.

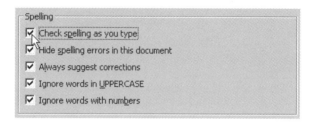

The spellchecker identifies suspect words, and shows
suggested alternatives. You can accept one of the suggestions,
edit the word yourself, or leave the original unchanged.

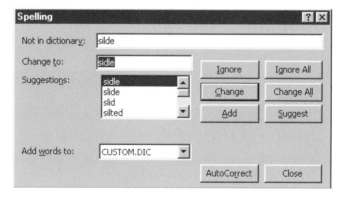

The spellchecker will not find incorrect spellings that are
themselves valid words (such as 'form' instead of 'from').

Chapter summary: so now you know

PowerPoint offers three *slide advance* methods: manual (operated by the presenter), automatic (after a specified time interval), or 'whichever comes first' (automatic with manual override). Automatic advance is often used in unaccompanied presentations that are left running in public areas.

A *transition* is a graphic effect that controls how one slide replaces another – for example, the new slide could appear to drop down from the top of the screen. You can control the speed with which PowerPoint runs your selected transition effect, and link a sound to the transition between slides.

An *animated slide* is one on which the elements are revealed gradually rather than all at once. These can help the presenter focus the audience's attention on each point in turn.

PowerPoint offers a set of 13 ready-to-go preset animations, some with associated sound effects, which you can quickly apply to your slides. You can customize preset animations as required. Options that you can modify include the order in which a slide's elements appear, the direction from which they appear, and the way in which previous elements are dimmed.

Animated elements can be bullet points, graphics such as lines or boxes, inserted pictures, and charts. You can also *animate charts* themselves, so that chart elements, such as the columns in a column chart, are displayed progressively rather than all at once.

PowerPoint's *spellchecker* can be run automatically so that it highlights suspect words as you type and edit slide text, or only as required.

CHAPTER 7

Presentations and file formats

In this chapter

How can you use information contained in PowerPoint presentations in files of other formats, such as web pages and graphics files? This section shows you how. You will also discover how to import spreadsheet data into PowerPoint slides.

PowerPoint comes with a range of design templates, which you can use as a basis for quickly creating other, similar presentations. You will learn how to apply the presupplied templates, and to create templates of your own.

New skills

At the end of this section you should be able to:
- Save PowerPoint presentation files in the following file formats: PowerPoint slideshows, earlier versions of PowerPoint, Excel, HTML (Web format), graphics (GIF or JPEG), Rich Text Format (RTF) and PowerPoint design templates
- Create a presentation based on a design template, and apply a design template to a new presentation
- Import cells and charts from Microsoft Excel into PowerPoint slides

New words

At the end of this section you should be able to explain the following terms:
- Design template

Saving your presentation as a slide show

You already know how to use Slide Show view to preview how your presentation will look to your audience. Another option is to save the presentation as a slide show, so that it always opens as a slide show, whether you open it within PowerPoint or directly from the desktop.

To save an open presentation as a slide show:

- Choose **File | Save As**.

- Click on the arrow to the right of the Save as type: box.

- Select PowerPoint Show.

PowerPoint saves the file with the extension .pps. Your original presentation file is unaffected. Exercise 7.1 provides an example.

Exercise 7.1: Saving a presentation as a slide show

1   If PowerPoint is not already open, open it now.

Open the ECDL presentation, with yellow text against a dark blue background, which you worked with in Chapter 6. You named it as KBpres2_yellow_on_blue.ppt or similar.

2 Choose **File | Save As**, and select the folder where you
want to save the file.

3 In the Save as type: box, select PowerPoint Show
(*.pps), accept or change the current file name, and
click **Save**.

4 Open Windows Explorer, and locate the folder where
you saved your slide show.

Backup of ECDL3_Mod1_April.wbk	360KB	Microsoft W
KBpres2_yellow_on_blue.pps	128KB	Microsoft Po
PowerPoint2000.htm	105KB	Microsoft HT
PowerPoint 2000 Tips.htm	28KB	Microsoft HT
PowerPoint2000_files		File Folder

5 Double-click the slide show. PowerPoint responds by
running the slide show on your screen.

When finished, close the slide show, but leave the
presentation open.

Working with earlier versions of PowerPoint

Each version of the Microsoft PowerPoint software includes
features that were not available in earlier versions. This means
that, while you can generally use a later version of the
software to open and work with a presentation that was
created in an earlier version, the reverse is not necessarily true.

You can save your PowerPoint 2000 presentations in the
file formats of previous versions of PowerPoint. You have
three main options:

- PowerPoint 97-2000 & 95 Presentation

- PowerPoint 95 Presentation

- PowerPoint 4.0

HTML (web) format

Web pages are created using the HTML file format. The file name extension of this format is .htm (or, sometimes, .html).

You can convert a complete PowerPoint presentation, a single slide, or a range of slides into HTML format, so that they can be displayed in a web browser such as Microsoft Internet Explorer or Netscape Navigator. Follow Exercise 7.2 to discover how.

Exercise 7.2: Saving a presentation in web format

1 Display the presentation that you worked on in Exercise 7.1.

2 Choose **File | Save As Web Page** and select the folder where you want to save the file.

To change the web page title (the text that appears in the title bar of the web browser), click **Change Title**, type the new title in the Page title box, and then click **OK**. When finished, click **Publish**.

3 On the Publish as Web Page dialog box display, select the values as shown below.

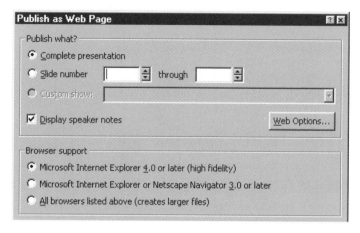

To see how the web version of your presentation looks in a web browser, select the checkbox at the bottom of the dialog box.

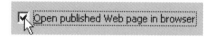

When finished, click **Publish**.

4 After a few seconds, PowerPoint will perform the file conversion, and open the first page of your presentation in the web browser. Click the slide titles on the left of the screen to navigate through the web-based version of your presentation. A sample page is shown opposite. You can close the file when finished.

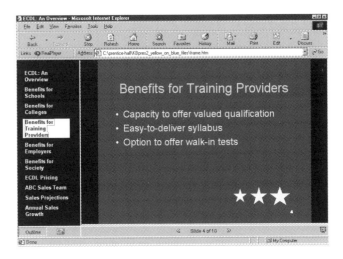

HTML options

PowerPoint offers a range of options when converting a presentation to HTML. To view the choices available for an open presentation:

- Choose **File | Save As Web Page** and select the folder where you want to save the file.

- Click **Publish** to display the Publish as Web Page dialog box, and click **Web Options** to display a dialog box with four tabs.

Your main options are as follows:

- **Slide navigation controls**: In Exercise 7.2, you accepted the default of white text against a black background.

- **Location of files**: Where do you want the supporting files located? The default is in a separate sub-folder.

- **Screen size**: The default is 800 × 600.

Saving slides as graphics

If you want to use your slides in other graphic programs, or within web pages, you can save them in one of the two common graphic formats: JPEG or GIF.

To save an open presentation as a graphic:

- Choose **File** | **Save As**.

- Select the folder where you want to save the file, and accept or amend the suggested file name.

- Click on the arrow to the right of the Save as type: box.

- Select GIF Graphics Interchange Format (*.gif) or JPEG File Interchange Format (*.jpg), and click **Save**.

- PowerPoint asks if you want to convert the entire presentation or just the current slide. Respond as appropriate.

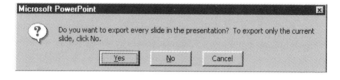

If you have selected all slides, you are shown another dialog box, similar to the one below.

PowerPoint saves the file(s) with the extension .gif or .jpg. Your original presentation file is unaffected.

Using PowerPoint slides in other applications

In general, you should not have to type information into one software application and then later type the same information into another application. For example, when you want to include in a Word document text that you have already entered to PowerPoint slides, you should not need to type it again.

To use text and/or graphics from a single slide, copy the item in PowerPoint (select it and press Ctrl+c), and paste it in Word (position the cursor and press Ctrl+v).

RTF format

To reuse an entire presentation in another application, the best option is to save the presentation in Rich Text Format (RTF). This is a format common to all Microsoft Office applications. The file name extension is .rtf.

To save an open presentation in RTF format:

- Choose **File | Save As**.

- Select the folder where you want to save the file, and accept or amend the suggested file name.

- Click on the arrow to the right of the Save as type: box.

- Select the Outline/RTF option, and click **Save**.

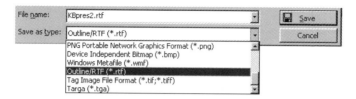

PowerPoint saves the file with the extension .rtf. Your original presentation file is unaffected.

Working with design templates

PowerPoint offers you the ability to save a presentation as a design template. You can then use the saved design template as a basis for quickly creating other, similar presentations.

To save an open presentation as design template:

* Choose **File | Save As.**

* Select the folder where you want to save the file, and accept or amend the suggested file name.

Typically, PowerPoint suggests that you save your design templates in the following folder:

> C:\Program Files\Microsoft Office\
> Templates\Presentation Designs

* Click on the arrow to the right of the Save as type: box.

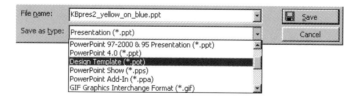

* Select the Design Template option, and click **Save.**

PowerPoint saves the design template with the extension .pot. Your original presentation file is unaffected. The next time you want to create a presentation, you can start with that saved design template and all the slides will take on its characteristics.

Design template

> *A PowerPoint file, containing a colour scheme and slide master with font settings, and possibly built-in graphics and text, which can be applied to a presentation. Design template files end in .pot.*

Presupplied design templates

In addition to design templates that you may create yourself, PowerPoint comes with a wide range of professionally designed templates. You can use the design templates as supplied, or amend them according to your particular needs or taste, or to your company identity scheme, and save them for later reuse.

To view PowerPoint's presupplied design templates:

- Choose **File | New**.

- On the New Presentation dialog box, click the Design Templates tab.

- Click once on the various templates listed to display a preview on the right of the dialog box.

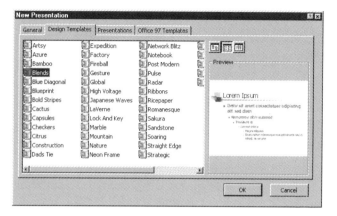

- When finished, click **Cancel**.

You are offered a choice of design templates only when you create a presentation with the **File | New** command, and not when you create a presentation by clicking the New button on the toolbar.

Design templates may contain colour schemes, and slide masters with font formatting and, optionally, built-in text and graphics.

Applying a design template

You can apply a design template to a presentation in either of two ways:

- **New presentation**: Create the presentation using the **File | New** command, and select the required design template from the list displayed.

- **Existing presentation**: Choose **Format | Apply Design Template**, and select the required design template from the list displayed.

When you apply a design template to an existing presentation, the slide master and colour scheme of the new template replace any slide master and colour scheme contained in the presentation.

Exercise 7.3: Applying a design template

1 Display the presentation that you worked on in Exercise 7.2.

2 In Normal view, choose **Format** | **Apply Design Template** to display the template choices available.

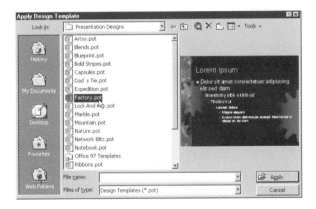

3 For this exercise, select the Factory.pot template, and click **Apply**.

4 Switch to Slide Show view to see the result. Pretty cool, eh?

5 Switch back to Normal view, and experiment further with other design templates.

6 When finished, choose **File** | **Save As**, and save the presentation with a name that indicates its design template. If your initials are KB, for example, save it as KBpres2_factory.ppt. Close your presentation, but do not close PowerPoint.

Importing spreadsheets and charts

In previous sections of this module you learnt how to import pictures and sounds to your slides. PowerPoint also allows you to import numerical data and charts from spreadsheets.

In Exercise 7.4 you will create a new presentation and import data from an Excel worksheet to it. And in Exercise 7.5, you will import an Excel chart to the presentation.

Exercise 7.4: Importing an Excel worksheet

1   Open Microsoft Excel. In a new workbook, enter the information shown.

	A	B	C
1	**River**	**Length (km)**	**Location**
2	Nile	6693	North/East Africa
3	Amazon	6436	South America
4	Yangtze	6378	China
5	Huang He	5463	China
6	Ob-Irtysh	5410	Russia
7			

rivers.xls

Save the workbook with the file name rivers.xls.

2   Switch to PowerPoint, choose **File | New**, select the design template called Bold Stripes, and click **OK**.

3   On the AutoLayout dialog box shown, select Title Slide, click **OK**, and type the text as shown on the next page.

4   Insert a second slide by clicking the New Slide button on the toolbar, selecting the AutoLayout named Title Only, and clicking **OK**.

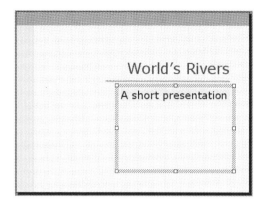

5　In the top placeholder of your second slide, enter the following text:

Longest Rivers

Click anywhere outside the top placeholder to deselect it.

6　Choose **Insert | Object**. On the dialog box shown, select the Create from file button, and click **Browse**.

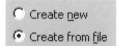

7　On the next dialog box, navigate to the folder where you saved the rivers.xls Excel file, select the file, and click **OK**. You are returned to the previous dialog box.

8　Click **OK** to close the first dialog box. The Excel worksheet is inserted on your slide.

Reposition and resize the imported worksheet until your slide looks as shown.

9 Save your presentation with an appropriate name. If your initials are KB, for example, call it KB_rivers.ppt.

You can work with the imported worksheet as you would any imported picture. For example, you can place a border or shadow around it, and copy it to other slides or the slide master. A worksheet included on the slide master appears on every slide of the presentation.

To change the content or appearance of the worksheet, double-click it, and use the Excel menus and toolbars displayed. To deselect the worksheet, click anywhere on the slide outside it.

Exercise 7.5: Importing an Excel chart

1 Display the Excel worksheet that you created and saved in Exercise 7.4.

2 Select the cell range A1:B6 and click the Chart Wizard button on the toolbar.

Excel's Chart Wizard button

	A	B	C
	River	**Length (km)**	**Location**
1			
2	Nile	6693	North/East Africa
3	Amazon	6436	South America
4	Yangtze	6378	China
5	Huang He	5463	China
6	Ob-Irtysh	5410	Russia

rivers.xls

3 On the first Chart Wizard dialog box, select a chart type of bar chart, and click **Next**.

4 On the second and third Chart Wizard dialog boxes, accept the default values and click **Next**. On the fourth dialog box, click **Finish**. Excel creates the chart on your worksheet.

5 With the chart selected, copy it to the clipboard, click the New button on the Excel Standard toolbar, and paste the chart in the new workbook. Save the workbook as rivers_chart.xls. You can now close Excel.

6 Switch to PowerPoint, and display the rivers presentation that you created in the previous exercise in Normal view.

7 Insert a third slide by clicking the New Slide button on the toolbar, selecting the AutoLayout named Blank, and clicking **OK**.

8 Choose **Insert | Object**. On the dialog box shown, select the Create from file button, and click **Browse**.

9 On the next dialog box, navigate to the folder where you saved the rivers_chart.xls Excel file, select the file, and click **OK**. You are returned to the previous dialog box.

10 Click **OK** to close the first dialog box. The Excel chart is inserted on your slide.

Reposition and resize the imported chart until your slide looks as shown.

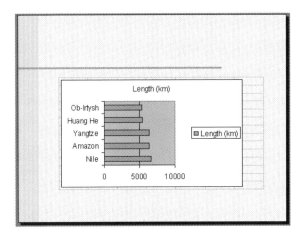

11 Save and close your presentation.

You may now save and close any open presentations, and close PowerPoint. You have completed the ECDL *Presentations* module congratulations!

Chapter summary: so now you know

To help you share your files with others, PowerPoint 2000 allows you to save your presentations in a file format other than its own. The options include: earlier versions of Microsoft PowerPoint, HTML (the web page file format), graphics files (GIF and JPEG), and Rich Text Format (RTF).

You can also save a presentation as a *slide show*, so that it always opens as a ready-to-run slide show, whether you open it within PowerPoint or directly from the desktop. PowerPoint slide show files end with the extension .pps.

Another option is to save a presentation as a *design template*, which you can then use as a basis for quickly creating other, similar presentations. Design templates may contain colour schemes, and slide masters with font formatting and, optionally, built-in text and graphics.

In addition to design templates that you may create yourself, PowerPoint comes with a wide range of professionally designed templates. You can use the design templates as supplied, or amend them according to your particular needs or taste, or to your company identity scheme, and save them for later reuse.

You can insert *spreadsheet* data, both numbers and charts, in a PowerPoint presentation. You can resize, reposition, place borders and shadows around, and copy-and-paste imported spreadsheet objects as you would imported pictures.